–

The Lost Dream

Urban Life and Urban Landscape Series

ZANE L. MILLER AND HENRY D. SHAPIRO, GENERAL EDITORS

MANSEL G. BLACKFORD

The Lost Dream

BUSINESSMEN AND CITY PLANNING

ON THE PACIFIC COAST

1890–1920

▼

OHIO STATE UNIVERSITY PRESS

COLUMBUS

Much of chapter 4 appeared in "Civic Groups, Political Action, and City Planning in Seattle, 1892–1915," *Pacific Historical Review* 49 (November 1980): 557–80. Much of chapter 5 appeared in "The Lost Dream: Businessmen and City Planning in Portland, Oregon, 1903–1914," *Western Historical Quarterly* 15 (January 1984): 39–56.

Library of Congress Cataloging-in-Publication Data

Blackford, Mansel G., 1944–
  The lost dream : businessmen and city planning on the Pacific
Coast, 1890–1920 / Mansel G. Blackford.
    p.   cm. — (Urban life and urban landscape series)
  Includes bibliographical references (p.   ) and index.
  ISBN 0-8142-0589-5 (alk. paper)
  1. City planning—Pacific States—History. 2. City planning—
Pacific States—Citizen participation—History. 3. Businessmen—
Pacific States—History. I. Title. II. Series.
HT167.5.A18B53   1992
307.1'26'0979—dc20   92–16405
                                                          CIP

Text and jacket design by James F. Brisson.
Type set in California by Connell-Zeko, Kansas City, MO.
Printed by Thomson-Shore, Dexter, MI.

The paper in this book meets the guidelines for permanence and durability of the Committee on Production Guidelines for Book Longevity of the Council on Library Resources. ⊛

9 8 7 6 5 4 3 2 1

For my wife, Victoria,

the circle closes

▼

CONTENTS

ILLUSTRATIONS

ix

MAPS

ACKNOWLEDGMENTS

My concern with the history of Pacific Coast cities is long-standing. Work as a graduate student with Professor Otis Pease at the University of Washington and Professor Gunther Barth at the University of California, Berkeley, first attracted me to the field. As a faculty member at The Ohio State University over the past two decades, I have found in the study of the roles businessmen played in the development of the urban West a vehicle by which to pursue varied interests in the history of cities, businesses, and frontiers.

Many people have aided me in preparing this volume. I have benefited from correspondence and conversations with Professors Carl Abbott, Stephen Erie, William Issel, Christine Rosen, Marc Weiss, and William Wilson. Several of my colleagues at The Ohio State University have helped me. I have enjoyed discussing this project with Professors William Childs, K. Austin Kerr, and Richard Hopkins and have benefited from their knowledge of urban history and the history of government-business relations in modern America. I would also like to thank Professor John Burnham for reading and commenting upon an earlier draft of this study. The anonymous reader for this press provided valuable suggestions about how my study might best be revised for publication. I would especially like to thank Professors Henry D. Shapiro and Zane L. Miller, the general editors of the Urban Life and Urban Landscape Series published by The Ohio State University Press, for their very careful readings of earlier drafts of this manuscript; their perceptive comments have greatly improved my work for publication. I would also like to thank Marjorie Haffner for her many secretarial skills used in preparing this manuscript.

Librarians and archivists at the University of Washington, the Oregon Historical Society, the Portland City Archives, the University of Oregon, and the Bancroft Library deserve my thanks. I would also like to thank The Ohio State University for three research grants in the 1970s and 1980s that supported much of my work on this project.

I remain, of course, solely responsible for the ultimate contents of this study.

Introduction

City Planning, Businessmen, and Scholars

▼

In the 1890s, residents of Pacific Coast cities—Seattle, Portland, Oakland, San Francisco, and Los Angeles in particular—mounted numerous significant, but disjointed, improvement efforts. During the first two decades of the twentieth century, the Progressive Era, their efforts coalesced into city planning movements. Pacific Coast urbanites considered adopting what they thought were comprehensive city plans encompassing harbor improvements, new street and transportation facilities, civic centers, and parks and boulevards. While many groups enhanced the planning movements, businessmen were usually the leaders and major supporters of planning.

Although city planning had diverse roots, much of it originated with businessmen because they viewed planning as a means to shape their urban environments both economically and socially. Businessmen remained strong supporters of the city planning efforts as the planning movements unfolded. Working through both established political channels and newly formed bodies outside of those channels, they played important roles in the planning movements as they matured. As the planning campaigns evolved, businessmen found themselves joined and opposed by others—professionals (especially architects, engineers, and lawyers), politicians, and workers. Businessmen worked for their goals in political arenas. Politics lay at the heart of planning: the proposed city plans were accepted or rejected in citywide elections in which, to be successful, businessmen had to convince others to vote with them.

In Pacific Coast cities, the politics of planning was pluralistic, but pluralistic only within certain limits.[1] That is, no single group completely dominated the political processes involving city planning, but neither did everyone have equal access to those processes.[2] Business organizations played the largest roles; but other bodies—groups of architects and engineers, labor organizations, and neighborhood improvement associations—were also significant. On the other hand, some people had almost no voice in how city planning developed. Once employed—sometimes engaged by the city governments, but often hired directly by the business groups— city planners initially drafted their plans with little input from others. Preliminary versions of the plans were then discussed with the public, and some revisions were made. But how were the plans discussed? Usually, representatives of various business, professional, neighborhood, and labor groups met with the planners to review details of the plans and suggest changes. Reflecting the organizational thrust of much of twentieth-century American life, only people belonging to recognized associations usually had access to the planners. Members of ethnic minorities and unorganized workers were generally excluded from the discussions. Only when it came time to vote could such people express their opinions in a meaningful way, and then only if they were registered voters.

Businessmen of nearly all sorts were active at one time or another in the planning movements. Real estate men, bankers, newspaper men, and industrialists played roles in the planning campaigns. Merchants were, however, of most significance and provided much of the backbone for the city planning movements— except in Los Angeles where real estate developers were particularly significant. Their importance should be expected, for Pacific Coast cities developed mainly as commercial centers, and merchants saw in city planning—both in the general idea of planning and in the specific improvements they imagined would result from planning—a way to elevate their metropolises above rival cities.

For merchants, planning seemed to promise both progress for their cities and profits for their purses. This study thus differs in emphasis from those that have stressed the importance of real estate interests, housing reformers, and professional landscape architects as the catalysts of changes in city planning. To be sure, they were all significant. In Pacific Coast cities, however, merchants were of more central importance.[3]

That businessmen were involved in city planning should not be surprising. Some businessmen have often worked on their own or with government officials in twentieth-century planning efforts when they have perceived the advantages of planning. Many businessmen were active participants in the development of federal and state regulation of the American economy in the Progressive Era. Businessmen remained active in various planning efforts during the 1920s and were deeply involved in New Deal activities during the 1930s. As some accepted conservative Keynesian economic ideas in the 1940s, 1950s, and 1960s, business leaders continued their engagement in planning in the postwar years. Far from being simply staunch individualists, many businessmen looked to planning as one way to try to stabilize their economic environments.[4]

Businessmen, City Growth, and City Planning

Pacific Coast cities were quickly growing in the late nineteenth and early twentieth centuries; and with their development came both opportunities and problems for their residents, especially their business leaders. From small villages in the mid-nineteenth century, the Pacific Coast centers emerged only one or two generations later as booming metropolises. With diverse populations dispersed over large areas, the rapid growth of the cities challenged attempts by business leaders to maintain their influence over them. At the same time, even as they became part of America's national urban network, the cities remained tied to Pacific Coast developments. Even as they won national recognition for

3

themselves as centers more substantial than mining towns and lumber camps, the cities came into increasing conflict with each other for economic control over the Pacific Coast—a rivalry that disturbed established relations among the region's merchants, financiers, and industrialists. It was in that context of economic and social flux that businessmen turned to city planning. Although the resulting plans were the products of what contemporary Americans called the "city beautiful" movement, they were more than attempts to beautify the cities. They were designed to solve problems and take advantage of opportunities that the businessmen thought their cities faced.

First and foremost, businessmen—especially merchants, but also bankers and industrialists—sought to heighten the economic power and reputations of their cities, and thus their own individual economic positions. For them city planning was both a defensive and offensive weapon: a means to defend their cities' positions in the intercity contests that were developing on the Pacific Coast, while also extending their economic reach. Trade, industry, people, and capital would migrate to properly planned cities, business leaders believed. City planning was in their minds a tool by which they might win the urban sweepstakes of the Pacific Coast. Merchants were particularly concerned about the opening of the Panama Canal. The imminent completion of the canal heightened an already well-developed sense of urban rivalry on the Pacific Coast, as merchants in each city hoped to reap what they thought would be untold benefits from the canal, at the expense of their neighbors.

More generally, through the civic improvements that they anticipated would flow from planning, businessmen sought to gain national recognition for their cities. They wanted them to be accepted fully as parts of America's urban network. Civic pride was a large part of the planning efforts. Business leaders in Oakland caught well that feeling when they urged the passage of a bond issue as a way of signaling to the "outside world" that their metropolis had "taken up her march on the high road of progress" and was about to assume "her proper place among cities."[5] Civic pride could, businessmen thought, have practical benefits. Beautiful and well-planned metropolises would attract new settlers, businesses, and capital. Beauty and economic growth would develop hand in hand.

Social objectives mixed with the economic goals. Through planning, business leaders tried to maintain and increase their social and cultural influence in their cities. Businessmen saw planning, with its espousal of civic pride and civic patriotism, as a potent means by which to buttress their social as well as their economic power. A lessening of social conflict and the uniting of dispersed neighborhoods were important agendas for those involved in city planning. Socially united cities, business leaders believed, would progress more rapidly than those rent by schisms. Thus, a San Francisco merchant lamented in 1909 that his city did "not display the same spirit of unity on local public questions" as did Seattle and blamed the "faction-torn" condition of his city for its lack of progress relative to that of its northern rival.[6]

Both optimism and pessimism permeated the thoughts of the businessmen involved in planning: they were two sides of the same coin. Business leaders in all of the Pacific Coast cities were optimistic about the future of their metropolises, *if* proper actions were taken. They were pessimistic, however, in believing that if such actions were not taken (and not taken quickly), their cities would fall behind their Pacific Coast rivals and metropolises across the nation to become merely second- or third-rate centers. Similarly, businessmen saw bright, harmonious futures for their cities, if only other groups could be persuaded to follow their lead in city planning.

Scholars and City Planning

During the past generation, historians have reevaluated progressivism. Beginning with studies in the 1950s and 1960s, historians increasingly have stressed the complexity of the progressive movement, seeing it as an attempt to reorder American life in the wake of the social and economic disruptions resulting from industrialization, the rise of big business, and the development of large cities.[7] City planning campaigns were often associated with progressivism on the Pacific Coast. Many of the general goals of the progessives, especially the desire to reestablish a sense of order and morality in America, were shared by the businessmen engaged in planning efforts. Moreover, many of the businessmen and business organizations involved in planning were active in the progressive movements in their cities.

An interpretation known as the organizational synthesis, first put forward in the 1970s, has helped conceptualize late nineteenth and early twentieth century American history in terms of the growing organization of life and thought.[8] That approach emphasizes the spread of bureaucratic organizations, the growth of professions, and a heightened awareness of a need for order and efficiency as the themes best explaining the course of American history in the late nineteenth and early twentieth centuries. Organizations had, of course, existed earlier; but their scale and scope increased dramatically after about 1850. Criticism of the organizational synthesis developed in the mid-1980s. Some scholars claimed that its description of modern America embodied "an unmistakable aura of inevitability, a sense that in its broad outlines at least, what has happened had to happen." The approach, its critics asserted, did not allow enough room in history to protest movements and thus "consigns the experiences of vast segments of society to the periphery of historical analysis and, in the end, leaves incomplete our view of modern America."[9]

The Pacific Coast city planning experience suggests that, its critics notwithstanding, the organizational synthesis approach offers a fruitful way to think about the evolution of late nineteenth and early twentieth century America. It was primarily through the work of their organizations, usually voluntary associations, that businessmen and others worked for and against city planning. Chambers of commerce, merchant bodies, architectural and engineering associations, neighborhood improvement groups, and labor organizations provided the vehicles through which planning advocates and opponents played out their ideas. Moreover, concerns about making urban life more efficient, more orderly, and more subject to the desires of planning professionals ran through the city planning movements.

The development of large cities constituted a major aspect of the modernization of the United States, and how Americans sought to shape their urban environments through planning has been a topic under investigation by a generation of historians. Writing in the 1960s, scholars prepared encyclopedic accounts of the history of city planning in America.[10] Their works pointed the way for more detailed research on the subject. Less wide-ranging studies, written primarily in the 1970s, examined the origins of the city planning movement. Those works showed that early city planning arose from diverse sources, ranging from municipal art movements to the efforts of engineers to design new urban sewer systems.[11] They reached less agreement, however, about the extent to which the city beautiful movement came to grips with the social and economic difficulties urbanites faced.[12]

In the 1980s, scholars investigated more fully the questions of causation in the development of city planning, the political conflicts surrounding the unfolding of planning campaigns, and the results of the planning efforts. Historians and social scientists renewed their interest in the history of city planning, and approached the topic from different points of view. A growing concern over the perceived failures of American cities in particular led scholars to reexamine the origins and growth of the nation's city planning movement.

Much of the interest initially originated with those who came to the topic from a Marxist or New-Left approach, deeply disillusioned with American society, politics, and institutions. Christine Boyer found that in the first two decades of the twentieth century planning was directed at imposing social discipline upon an unruly urban populace and providing city services needed for private commercial and industrial growth.[13] In the same vein, Richard Fogelsong saw in planning the unfolding of two contradictions: "the contradiction between the social character of land and its private ownership and control" and "a contradiction between the need to socialize the control of urban space . . . and the danger of truly socializing, that is, democratizing, the control of urban land."[14] Fogelsong found in early twentieth century planning "an attempt to create social and moral cohesiveness in a heterogeneous urban society in which face-to-face methods of social control had proven unworkable."[15]

One need not share Boyer's and Fogelsong's orientation to agree that some of the planning movement was elitist in leadership and that it sought to impose the values of middle-class businessmen and professionals upon other segments of society. Their analysis is, however, incomplete. It obscures much of the complexity of the planning movement, and particularly why it was only partially successful. Businessmen were far from unified in

7

their approaches to planning. They came into conflict with other groups of businessmen and with other professionals much more frequently than Boyer and Fogelsong suggest, and those divisions greatly weakened planning efforts.

Less ideologically motivated have been the recent works of other scholars. In her examination of how Chicago, Boston, and Baltimore rebuilt after being destroyed by catastrophic fires, Christine Rosen has shown that, by eliminating old structures, natural disasters can clear the way for urban redevelopment. She has also demonstrated, however, that disasters may not remove all of the limitations to redevelopment, for political barriers may remain. Rosen's study is particularly compelling for suggesting a way of viewing events in San Francisco after that city's earthquake and fire in 1906.[16] Stanley Schultz has surveyed improvement and planning efforts in the nineteenth century, focusing on the work of engineers to devise sewer and water systems. Here originated, Schultz has argued, the source of city planning efforts in the twentieth century. Looking briefly at the city beautiful movement, Schultz has found in it far more "than mere aesthetics." Like the progressive movement—of which, according to Schultz, it was a part—the city beautiful movement sought to "restore order to a chaotic society, to render more efficient the functioning of all human endeavors, and above all, to reinstate morality as the core of human behavior."[17]

The City Beautiful Movement by historian William Wilson offers the most thorough examination of city planning during the Progressive Era. Examining planning movements in Harrisburg, Denver, Seattle, Dallas, and Kansas City, Wilson concludes that the efforts were realistic attempts to handle urban problems. In their planning work "middle- and upper-middle-class Americans attempt[ed] to refashion their cities into beautiful, functional entities."[18] The city beautiful movement was, Wilson has observed, at one and the same time "a cultural, aesthetic, political, and environmental movement" that achieved considerable success.[19] In addition to its physical improvements, the movement gave Americans a sense that comprehensive planning was possible. Taking an approach at variance with those of Boyer and Fogelson, Wilson views planning in the early twentieth century as a positive and optimistic effort to remake the nation's cities.

The study of planning also contributes to our understanding of the roles cities played in the development of American frontiers, especially in the trans-Mississippi West.[20] Scholars have recognized for some time now that cities were crucial to the opening of frontiers to settlement, and solid urban biographies exist for a number of Pacific Coast cities.[21] Historians have also prepared broader studies emphasizing the significance of cities in the regional development of the Far West.[22] Recent interest has focused on western cities in the late nineteenth and early twentieth centuries and, in particular, the question of to what degree their development may have differed from that of their eastern counterparts.[23]

Particularly important have been the studies of Gunther Barth and Lawrence Larson. Writing about Denver and San Francisco, Barth has postulated that those cities developed differently from urban centers elsewhere. They grew up very rapidly as "instant cities," telescoping into just one or two generations the economic, social, and cultural developments that most cities required much longer to attain. Barth asserts, "The rapid rise of San Francisco and Denver distinguished them from most other American cities, which matured from settlement to town over many decades and even centuries."[24] Moreover, because of the rapidity of their growth, Denver and San Francisco possessed much more fluid social, political, and cultural structures and norms than other metropolises. To the contrary, Larson has found in his study of the history of twenty-four western cities, including Denver and San Francisco, that western cities were similar to their eastern counterparts in most respects. He concludes, "In building cities western pioneers followed what they understood best . . . [and] they rigidly copied older concepts of urban planning."[25]

Seattle, Portland, Oakland, and Los Angeles—like San Francisco and Denver—grew up very rapidly, perhaps justifying the application of the label "instant city" to them. More than any other single factor, their runaway growth and its influence on businessmen led to the development of planning movements in those cities. Nonetheless, the planning efforts were very similar to those that arose in eastern and midwestern cities at about the same time. In fact, most of the plans were prepared by well-known eastern planners who paid scant attention to the western settings of the Pacific Coast cities.

The study of Pacific Coast city planning enhances our comprehension of how businessmen related to their changing social and economic environments. America's foremost business historians have examined the relationships between businessmen and their environments in different ways. In a number of broad-ranging studies, Thomas Cochran has looked at national developments, illustrating well the growth of a business culture in the United States.[26] More interested in the evolution of the business firm and its management, Alfred D. Chandler, Jr., has written extensively about the rise of big business in America.[27] Much remains to be learned about how businessmen related to their regional and local environments.[28] Findings about the roles businessmen played in the planning movements of Pacific Coast cities suggest strongly that, just as they sought to make their business environments more predictable through the adoption of modern management techniques for their firms, so, too, did businessmen try to use city planning to stabilize their urban environments. Just as they were coming to view themselves as professionals and experts in the management of their companies, so, too, did business leaders view planners as experts in the running of cities.

The Scope of This Study

This work examines the genesis of city planning, looks at how businessmen and others sought through politics to put their ideas into practice, and examines the results of the planning efforts. Most importantly, this volume contributes to our understanding of the Progressive era in American history and the politics of city planning as part of the political ferment of that period. Secondarily, it adds to our comprehension of the nature of western cities, especially the degree to which they were similar or different from their eastern counterparts. Finally, this volume increases our understanding of the roles businessmen have played in shaping American society and culture.

Chapter 1 sets the stage for the examination of city planning by analyzing the social and economic development of Seattle, Portland, Oakland, San Francisco, and Los Angeles. Those five metropolises are logical cities to compare in their planning efforts, for in their economic roots and in their social origins—and how these changed over time—they shared many characteristics. While those centers participated in the spread of a national network of cities in America, the fact that they grew up on the Pacific Coast lent a commonality to their development.

San Francisco, the subject of chapter 2, was one of the first American cities for which a Progressive-Era city plan was drafted. Moreover, because of the destruction caused by its 1906 earthquake and fire, San Francisco had an unusual chance to embrace planning as a guide for its growth in the twentieth century. Why San Franciscans passed up the opportunity to construct a new planned city reveals a great deal about the political, as opposed to the physical, limitations to city planning in the United States.

Chapters 3, 4, and 5 investigate the evolution of planning in the other major cities of the Pacific Coast. Chapter 3 looks at planning in Oakland and Los Angeles. Charles Mumford Robinson prepared plans for both cities. Oakland and Los Angeles also pioneered in the use of zoning as a planning tool. Turning from California to the Pacific Northwest, chapter 4 examines the course of events in Seattle. Seattleites considered the most highly engineered, the most technically proficient, plan drawn up for a Pacific Coast city, only to reject it in the end. Chapter 5 looks at Portland. The voters of Portland approved the adoption of a city plan as a guide for the development of their metropolis, the only people on the Pacific Coast to do so; but they soon ignored the plan in the rapid expansion of their city.

Finally, chapter 6 draws conclusions about the nature of city planning on the Pacific Coast. The chapter assesses what was and was not accomplished and compares the experiences of Pacific Coast cities with planning to those of cities elsewhere in the nation.

The Pacific Coast

WASHINGTON

Seattle

Portland

OREGON

ID

NV

San Francisco Oakland

CALIFORNIA

Los Angeles

AZ

Pacific
Ocean

1

From Village to Metropolis

▼

Writing in 1878, the historian John S. Hittell described San Francisco as the "leading center of population, commerce, industry, wealth, luxury . . . intellectual, political and financial activity" of the Pacific Coast. San Francisco was, he observed, "the most brilliant center of civilization in the bosom of the North Pacific and the metropolis of the western coast of the United States."[1] As Hittell suggested, cities like San Francisco were supremely important in the development of the Pacific Coast. Urban centers acted as catalysts transforming the back country into settled areas. San Francisco, Oakland, Los Angeles, Seattle, and Portland led the growth of the Pacific Coast to become in the early twentieth century one of the more heavily urbanized sections of the United States.[2] Even as they altered the Pacific Coast, the cities themselves changed. As they grew, they became more and more spatially dispersed and increasingly diverse in terms of the social and economic backgrounds of their residents.

While rapidly growing and changing, the Pacific Coast cities were hardly unique. The United States was becoming a distinctly urban nation in the years between the Civil War and World War I. Through transportation improvements, especially the telegraph and railroad, America became more and more a nation of interconnected large cities, in which regional and national urban networks grew.[3] The story of the rise of Pacific Coast cities is, in part, an account of the roles they played in the development of urban networks in the United States in general and in the Far West in particular.

Economic Growth

From the outset, the Pacific Coast grew up as largely urban, one of the more heavily urbanized regions in the United States.[4] In fact, Pacific Coast cities developed rapidly in the late nineteenth century—so quickly that some of them differed fundamentally in their early development from the evolution of most other cities in the United States. They were "instant cities," centers compressing the process of urbanization normally requiring many decades to complete into just one or two generations.[5] Such development was most pronounced in San Francisco (and beyond the Pacific Coast in Denver and Chicago), but all of the other major Pacific Coast cities shared to some degree in that pattern of growth.[6]

San Francisco quickly became the preeminent commercial center of the Pacific Coast. Possessing one of the two good natural harbors on the coast (Seattle had the other), San Francisco had

Population Growth in Pacific Coast Cities

	1890	1900	1910
SAN FRANCISCO	298,997	342,782	416,912
OAKLAND	48,682	66,960	150,174
LOS ANGELES	50,395	102,479	319,198
SEATTLE	42,837	80,671	237,194
PORTLAND	46,385	90,426	207,214

well-established trade connections with the Atlantic Coast, Europe, Mexico, Latin America, Hawaii, and the Far East even before the discovery of gold at Sutter's Mill in 1848. Nonetheless, it was the tremendous expansion of commerce resulting from the gold rush that provided the city with its initial spurt of growth. As the jumping-off point for the diggings, San Francisco controlled the gold rush of the late 1840s and early 1850s. While San Francisco's basic economic function as a transshipment point did not change from Mexican to American times, the goods handled did. Gold became the chief export, reaching $54 million in value at its highest point in 1853. Imports became increasingly varied: lumber from Maine, agricultural goods and more lumber from the Pacific Northwest, flour from Chile, silk and rice from China, and manufactured products from the cities of the East Coast.[7] From a hamlet of fewer than five hundred residents in 1846, San Francisco became a boomtown of fifty thousand a scant ten years later.

By 1870 San Francisco was a city of nearly 150,000; and ten years later it had become a metropolis of 234,000, the ninth largest city in the United States. Trade continued to drive San Francisco's growth. Well into the late nineteenth century, the city controlled nearly all of the commerce within California, most of the coastal trade of the Pacific Coast, and much of the foreign trade of the region.[8] San Francisco emerged as the financial center of the Pacific Coast. The actions of William Ralston, the president of the Bank of California, force-fed the growth of San Francisco in the early and mid-1870s. An urban entrepreneur, Ralston used bank funds and his own income, both derived from the control the bank exerted over the silver mines of Nevada's Comstock Lode, to finance the construction of theaters, hotels, carriage works, woolen mills, sugar refineries, and furniture factories in San Francisco. Ever an optimist, Ralston eventually overreached himself, however. In 1875 the Bank of California was forced to close its doors, and Ralston was found dead a short time later, an apparent suicide.[9]

Merchants, bankers, and real estate men—not manufacturers—made early San Francisco. Yet, although not as important as commerce in San Francisco's development, manufacturing rose in significance as time passed. As early as 1860, San Francisco ranked ninth among American cities in the value of its manufactures, but 52 percent of all of the manufacturing in the city had to do with the refining of gold and silver. During the next five decades, the city developed a more varied industrial base in food processing, the fabrication of clothing, ironmaking, and shipbuilding. By 1910 some 32 percent of the city's work force had manufacturing jobs, compared to 39 percent in trade and transportation.[10]

Across San Francisco Bay, Oakland grew up as a bedroom suburb of San Francisco, with many of its inhabitants embarking daily by ferry to work in the larger city. One real estate brochure of the 1880s claimed that "seven thousand San Francisco merchants own superb homes in Oakland and educate their children here." Oakland's residents prided themselves on the bucolic nature of their town. Streets lined with oak trees and beautiful real estate subdivisions won their praise and the accolades of visitors to their town. "We stopped at Oakland for the reason that we had heard so much of the beauty of the place," wrote a visitor from New York in 1880. "We found it beautiful indeed." A pamphlet distributed by the Board of Trade stressed the advantages of living in Oakland in terms of its climate, noting that "its atmosphere is pure, and at the same time mild; bracing, yet with an Italian softness."[11]

Oakland emerged as a major Pacific Coast city in the years 1890 through 1910. As late as 1890, Oakland possessed only one-sixth of the population of San Francisco, but two decades later Oakland was one-third the size its larger neighbor. By 1910 Oakland possessed three-quarters as many residents as Portland, three-fifths as many as Seattle, and one-half of the number living in Los Angeles. The Oakland Chamber of Commerce closed one of its meetings in 1906 with the simple statement, "Oakland is to be the metropolis of the West."[12] Both commercial and industrial developments lay behind Oakland's growth. Harbor improvements allowed Oakland to take over much of the coastal and foreign trade once going through San Francisco, until by 1910 about 30 percent of the freight tonnage passing through the Golden Gate was handled by Oakland merchants. Oakland also became a center of industry. The city had always possessed some local industries: breweries, canneries, and cotton mills. With better transportation links resulting from the improvements to their harbor and the entrance of additional railroads to their city, Oakland manufacturers were able to increase the scope of their operations. They benefited as well from the earthquake and fire that destroyed much of San Francisco in 1906, since many of the damaged city's industries relocated in relatively intact Oakland.[13]

Developments in Southern California seemed more difficult to explain. Writing in 1902, a San Francisco insuranceman wondered about the growth taking place in Los Angeles. Like many people of his time, he was baffled by the city's rapid expansion. Neither manufacturing, foreign trade, nor the possession of a productive hinterland seemed to lie behind the city's development. Like many other San Franciscans, however, he viewed Los Angeles as a growing threat to his city's hegemony over the Pacific Coast. As he put it in a business magazine:

> The oftener one visits Los Angeles the more certain he becomes that it is a freak creation. There is really no actual reason for its being—i.e. as a handsome big city. It is not a manufacturing town, nor a commercial city; neither has it a big productive area around it. . . . All the same there is no disputing the fact that it is here. A big fine-appearing city— architecturally infinitely superior to San Francisco or any other coast town.[14]

Far from being a new settlement when California entered the Union in 1850, Los Angeles was almost seventy years old; but there was little about the town that foreshadowed its development as a great metropolis. Los Angeles was a nondescript agricultural village of 1,610, geographically isolated from the rest of the United States. Nor did that status change quickly, for the gold rush passed Los Angeles by. Lacking San Francisco's good harbor and nearby natural resources, Los Angeles seemed destined to obscurity. In 1876 the town still possessed only six thousand inhabitants.[15]

The coming of the railroad changed the situation. In 1876 the residents of Los Angeles approved a $600,000 subsidy to attract the Southern Pacific Railroad. When the line was completed a few years later, Los Angeles possessed its first transcontinental connection, and a second was added when the Atchison, Topeka, and Santa Fe Railroad entered the town in 1883. To increase traffic the railroads sought to attract settlers and mounted a national advertising campaign that pictured Southern California as a Garden of Eden. Rate wars meant that cheap overland transportation was available (for a time in 1887 the cost of traveling from the

Mississippi Valley to Los Angeles was reduced to only one dollar).[16]

People came to Los Angeles in a series of booms. A health boom attracted many in the 1880s as they sought Southern California's year-long, mild, Mediterrean climate and natural beauty. With its "perpetual spring," Los Angeles was, its boosters declared, "a veritable sanitorium." Still others came to Los Angeles to retire. By 1910, 21 percent of the city's residents were over the age of fifty-five, a proportion considerably higher than the 14 to 17 percent in most American cities. The possibilities of growing fruit, especially oranges, drew others into the region. An oil boom beckoned to still more. By 1914 California had moved into first place among the oil-producing states of the nation, with much of the oil gushing from wells in Southern California.[17]

More significant than either oil or oranges was real estate speculation. Beginning in the 1880s, the work of subdividers eager to attract buyers advanced the economy of Los Angeles in a series of booms and busts. The interaction of immigrants with real estate men was the force that seemed to create in Los Angeles its insubstantial quality. The work of Henry Huntington was of special importance. In a manner similar to William Ralston several decades earlier in San Francisco, Huntington played the role of urban entrepreneur. Through his control of companies in a triad of interrelated industries—real estate, electric street railroads, and electric power generation—Huntington both built up Los Angeles and bolstered his private fortune during the first two decades of the twentieth century.[18] Only in the very late nineteenth and early twentieth centuries did Los Angeles start becoming a center for commerce and industry, and even then the activities of real estate developers remained more significant than those of merchants and manufacturers in the city's advance.[19]

What San Francisco was for the entire Pacific Coast, Portland was on a smaller scale for many years to the Pacific Northwest, the premier commercial city. Founded in 1844 on the banks of the Willamette River just upstream from its confluence with the Columbia River, Portland possessed valuable water connections to the Pacific Ocean. Portland's first significant burst of growth came with the gold rush to California. Abandoning the mines, some people settled in Oregon. More importantly, San Franciscans needed food grown in Oregon's rich Willamette Valley and lumber from the forests of the Pacific Northwest, and much of the trade in those goods passed through the hands of Portland's merchants. Through their control of that commerce and of local trade, Portland businessmen were able in the 1850s and 1860s to achieve dominance over their rivals in nearby communities, boosting their town to a position of regional power.[20]

Portland continued to develop as a commercial center for the next half century. When the demands of San Franciscans slackened, Portland merchants extended their reach for markets; and in that action they were aided by the coming of transcontinental railroads to their city in the 1870s and 1880s. The railroads helped Portland's business leaders both participate in America's growing national market and extend their sway over a regional hinterland reaching from Oregon into eastern Washington and parts of western Idaho and Montana.[21] As a center for increasingly diversified trade, Portland experienced steadier growth than Los Angeles or San Francisco for most of the nineteenth century and had a population reaching forty-six thousand by 1890.[22]

Growth soon accelerated. Portland's population doubled in the 1890s and then doubled again in the first decade of the twentieth century to reach 207,000. Much of Portland's development continued to be based on trade. The expansion of farming in western Oregon and the upper Columbian Basin led to a population increase of 500,000 in Portland's interior hinterland in the opening years of the twentieth century. Portland also benefited from a substantial increase in demand for Pacific Northwest lumber. Associated with the trade expansion was the growth of industry, as Portland businessmen set up furniture factories, canning plants, and flour mills to process the fruits of field and forest. Still more was involved. Portland became large enough to support manufacturing and service industries geared to its home market, which in turn helped set off a real estate boom that pushed the value of new building permits granted in Portland up 400 percent between 1905 and 1911. By 1910 Portland was in the midst of prosperity. There was, wrote one of the city's journalists, "no cloud on the horizon."[23]

Such optimism was partially misplaced, for Seattle was rapidly replacing Portland as the leading center of commerce, industry, and population in the Pacific Northwest. Founded in 1851 on Elliot Bay in Puget Sound, Seattle was in its early days a lumber

19

town, with San Francisco as its major market. An Indian scare, poor transportation links to the rest of the country, a scarcity of women (only twenty of its two hundred inhabitants in 1860 were women), and recurrent fires limited Seattle's growth. The town possessed only 3,533 inhabitants in 1880.[24]

Seattle's rapid development, like that of Los Angeles and Oakland, began when the city acquired rail connections to the Midwest and East. In the 1880s, Seattle secured indirect links through the Northern Pacific; and in 1893 the Great Northern designated Seattle as its western terminal point, giving Seattle direct connections to eastern markets.[25] The rail lines were completed just in time for Seattle to benefit from further developments in the 1890s. With much of the Great Lakes states cut over, America came to depend more heavily than before on the Pacific Northwest for its lumber; and Seattle, like Portland, helped supply that demand. Weyerhaueser Lumber made Seattle its new home as the firm moved west. Even more explosive, although also more short-lived, was the impact on Seattle of the gold rush to Alaska. Possessing a fine natural harbor and ambitious merchants, Seattle benefited more than San Francisco or Portland as an outfitting point for the North.[26] At the same time, local railroads opened coal mines and farming areas near Seattle. The exploitation of its regional hinterland was as important as the opening of national markets for Seattle's continuing development. Pushed by those events, Seattle's population reached forty-three thousand by 1890 and eighty-one thousand ten years later.[27]

Seattle's population then tripled to 237,000 in 1910. Much of the growth occurred as an extension of trends begun earlier. The lumber industry, a rich farming hinterland, and coastal and foreign trade remained important underpinnings in the city's development. In addition, new industries developed beyond the small-scale, local stage: shipbuilding, the salmon industry (Seattleites controlled the Alaskan as well as the local fishing industry), and ironmaking. Perhaps most importantly, as was taking place at about the same time in Portland, Seattle became a large enough market in and of itself to spur the growth of a wide variety of manufacturing and service businesses. As a result, Seattle's economy became more diversified than in earlier years.[28]

All of the Pacific Coast cities thus grew initially as commercial cities exploiting natural resources in the hinterlands at their command.[29] San Francisco received its boost from the gold rush to California, and Oakland initially fed upon San Francisco's development. Los Angeles benefited from a series of health, real estate, fruit-growing, and oil booms in Southern California. Portland and Seattle owed their growth to numerous causes, but most importantly to the control they exerted over the agricultural and lumber industries of the Pacific Northwest.

Commerce would long remain at the heart of the Pacific Coast cities, and, indeed, is still very important to them today. Unlike some eastern and midwestern cities, those on the Pacific Coast did not become national industrial centers. Commerce lay at their core into at least the 1920s. Nonetheless, the economies of the Pacific Coast cities became increasingly diversified with the passage of time. Industrial and service businesses developed to serve the growing populations of the cities and their hinterlands; and in some cases, most notably in that of San Francisco, the new businesses reached beyond local markets to regional and even national markets. In short, as time passed, Pacific Coast cities—like many cities elsewhere in the United States—moved beyond their origins to become complex centers of economic activity.

Spatial and Population Development

As the Pacific Coast cities developed, they spread outward to cover larger areas and their populations became more diverse. New methods of transportation, especially electric street railroads, enabled the cities to cover more and more land, just as was happening in urban centers elsewhere in America. At the same time, the movement of immigrants into some of the Pacific Coast cities and the differentiation of their economies led to division of the populations into distinct groups. Neighborhoods distinguished by race or income level formed. The growth of industry, however hesitant, also contributed to social divisions, as socioeconomic classes began developing. Social conflict, both real and perceived, came to characterize the cities, as people of different classes and backgrounds lived in spatially separated neighborhoods that seemed to have little in common.

San Francisco never possessed a socially homogeneous population. As a magnet for fortune-seekers of all sorts, the city attracted a diverse citizenry from the first, and that diversity persisted into the twentieth century.[30] In 1900, 30 percent of the city's population was foreign-born, and an additional 40 percent had parents who were born abroad. While 94 percent of the population was white (5 percent was Chinese or Japanese, and 0.5 percent black), many nationalities were represented—Irish, Germans, English, and Italians being the most common.[31] Socioeconomic divisions also separated San Franciscans. By the early twentieth century, San Francisco was the most heavily unionized city on the Pacific Coast, and one of the more heavily unionized in the United States. Labor-management conflict was common, often going beyond the lines of single crafts to pit workers against employers throughout the city almost as warring groups, especially from 1901 onward.[32]

Hemmed in by geographic barriers—San Francisco Bay to the north and east, high hills to the west—San Francisco was more densely populated than the other Pacific Coast cities, and in the 1870s and 1880s distinct neighborhoods grew up. Most lasted with only a few changes into the twentieth century: the South of Market District of young, unskilled men living in boardinghouses, the Mission District made up of skilled workers, often Irish, the Italian North Beach, Chinatown, the middle-class Western Addition, the upper-class Nob Hill and Pacific Heights, and so forth. In the early twentieth century tunnels were bored through the hills and streetcar lines built to open new areas to settlement—the Richmond District, a middle-class area, being the most notable. Neighborhood developments reinforced the economic and ethnic divisions perceived by some of San Francisco's business leaders, barriers they hoped to break down through city planning.[33]

Across San Francisco Bay, Oakland possessed a more homogeneous population. However, small black, Japanese, and Chinese populations established themselves, each living in its own part of town; and, as the city developed an industrial base, a wider variety of whites settled there. More noticeable than the development of ethnic neighborhoods was the growth of middle-class and upper-class areas—Piedmont, Montclair, Trestle Glen, the Crocker Highlands—within the existing city limits, a development made possible by the rapid adoption of the electric street railroad. Oakland also grew by annexation, especially in the years 1897 through 1910, when it acquired Temescal, Linda Vista, Peralta, Claremont, Fruitvale, Melrose, Fitchberg, and Elmhurst. Much less densely populated than San Francisco, Oakland covered sixty-three square miles by 1910, up from only a few square miles thirty years before.[34]

Like Oakland, Los Angeles had a more uniform population than San Francisco. In the nineteenth century native white Americans and immigrants from western Europe comprised most of the population of Los Angeles, but the city's population grew more diversified in the early twentieth century as Los Angeles attracted immigrants from southern and eastern Europe, Mexico, and Japan. Even so, only 4 percent of the population was nonwhite in 1910, and only 19 percent was composed of foreign-born whites. Much of the population was made up of farmers and small-town folk who moved from the Midwest or Great Plains to retire. As the historian Robert Fogelson has noted, the great majority of the residents of Los Angeles "fit well within the broad range of the middle class, had rural midwestern, or at least native American backgrounds."[35]

More than any other Pacific Coast city, Los Angeles sprawled. Real estate subdividers working with the owners of streetcar lines (often the same people, as in the case of Henry Huntington) led to an "unmatched residential dispersal" in Los Angeles. Already larger in area than its Pacific Coast rivals by 1910 (though still smaller in population than San Francisco), Los Angeles continued to outpace them in succeeding years. By 1930 Los Angeles trailed only New York in area among American cities, and it was nearly twice as large as the combined areas of San Francisco and Oakland.[36]

Sharper divisions among different segments of its citizenry accompanied Portland's growth. By 1910 about 21 percent of the city's residents were of foreign birth and another 25 percent were of foreign or mixed parentage. Immigrant neighborhoods developed. Jewish communities, which had long existed, increased in importance to the point that they had their own newspaper and a leader acknowledged as their mayor. One section of the city became the center of an Italian colony, and another was inhabited by Greek railroad workers. Substantial bodies of blacks, Chinese, and Japanese also lived in the town.[37]

23

When compared to the much more heavily unionized cities of San Francisco and Seattle, Portland was relatively free of labor-management strife. Like Los Angeles, Portland was known as a nonunion town. Nonetheless, organized labor increased its strength in Portland during the opening decade of the twentieth century. In 1908 the city's unions formed a Central Labor Council to coordinate their activities, and a few months later business leaders set up the Employers Association of Oregon in opposition. Growing class divisions found political outlets. In 1909 the Portland *Labor Press* led a successful drive to deprive a real estate developer of the city's mayoralty because his "administration, if he is elected, will be a riot of business, big business." Two years later, the Longshoremen's Union spearheaded a movement that organized the Workingmen's Political Club, which endorsed candidates with "the labor point-of-view" for election to city offices.[38]

Like most of the other Pacific Coast cities, Portland experienced rapid spatial expansion. In 1891 Portland, East Portland, and Albina consolidated, boosting Portland's area from seven to twenty-five square miles. During the next twenty years, the electric street railroad opened outlying areas to settlement; and, as real estate developers worked with the owners of streetcar companies, suburbs grew up. Particularly important was the growth of the area east of the Willamette River, for conflict between businessmen in that newly developing area with those in the long-established district west of the river would make it difficult for Portland's business community to reach agreements on city planning measures. At the same time, interurbans made Portland's downtown business district accessible to the residents of nearby communities. As those people began shopping in Portland, the economic bases of their towns eroded, and many of the formerly independent towns were annexed to Portland.[39]

Those developments increased Portland's size to nearly fifty square miles by 1915. The spatial growth segmented Portland physically, for it was haphazard. Despite a consolidation movement, Portland still possessed several competing streetcar lines serving the city in an uncoordinated manner in the early twentieth century. The city's geography, like that of Seattle and San Francisco, also made geographic unity difficult to achieve. High hills and the Willamette River divided parts of the metropolis.

As Seattle entered the twentieth century, its population lost whatever homogeneity it may have had when the city was a frontier town. As in Portland and Los Angeles, about 20 percent of Seattleites were of foreign birth in 1910. Most of the immigrants came from the German states in Seattle's early days; but many came from Scandinavia, Canada, China, and Japan as well. Ethnic neighborhoods grew up—a Chinatown, a Japantown, a Jewish area, a Little Italy, a Russian neighborhood, and Scandinavian enclaves—but they never assumed the importance of ethnic neighborhoods in San Francisco or in many eastern cities. Despite the influx of some foreigners, Seattle, like Los Angeles, maintained something of a midwestern flavor, with about one-quarter of its residents having been born in the Midwest and with many of its foreign-born inhabitants having lived there for substantial periods before moving on to Seattle.[40]

Although ethnicity became increasingly significant in segmenting Seattleites into different groups, occupational and economic status was of greater importance.[41] While some members of different groups were dispersed throughout Seattle, residential patterns based on occupation developed in the late nineteenth and early twentieth centuries. Moreover, like San Francisco, Seattle was heavily unionized and experienced much labor-management strife during the opening decades of the twentieth century. As in San Francisco and Portland, geographic features, hills and bodies of water, also helped define neighborhoods. Finally, Seattle greatly expanded its area by annexing many previously independent towns—Ballard, Wallingford, Georgetown, and others—in the late nineteenth and early twentieth centuries, making any sense of civic unity difficult to achieve.[42]

Urban Networks and
Intercity Rivalry

Cities have always been important in the development of the United States, but their rapid growth after the Civil War greatly increased their significance. As early as the 1840s and 1850s, according to the urban geographer Allan Pred, an urban network was fast arising. By those decades, he observed, "the total pattern of interurban relationships, or interdependencies, that either continued or appeared for the first time was complex to a degree that suggests a more than rudimentary integration among the expanding membership of the nation's city-system."[43] Other scholars have traced the emergence of such a network to the late nineteenth century. It was then, the urban historian Blake McKelvey has explained, that "a closely integrated galaxy of cities" grew up. In 1860 the United States possessed 141 centers of at least eight thousand inhabitants, but by 1910 the number of such towns and cities had increased nearly sixfold. By 1920, for the first time in the history of their nation, more Americans lived in towns and cities of twenty-five hundred or more inhabitants than resided on farms or in villages.[44]

Western cities were part of the urban network from their first days. San Francisco was connected to the East by sailing ships and was dependent upon eastern sources for all types of goods, from groceries to metal products. With the completion of transcontinental railroads to the Pacific Coast cities in the late nineteenth century, the centers became increasingly linked to national developments. Pacific Coast businessmen were proud of the growing roles their cities played in the national urban network. For them, it was a matter of some consequence that their cities be acknowledged as the equals of urban centers in the East and Midwest, for such recognition would, they thought, help them attract businesses and settlers. As a leading member of San Francisco's Chamber of Commerce explained in 1911, a time when the city's residents were considering civic improvements in preparation for the 1915 world's fair, "the eyes of the world are . . . upon San Francisco. Prospective real estate investors the world over are looking toward San Francisco . . . Let us prepare for our guests by cleaning house."[45]

If Pacific Coast cities were part of a growing national urban network, they nonetheless remained tied to their West Coast heritages. They were members of a regional network of cities and towns. In fact, as their hinterlands developed, Pacific Coast cities became more and more active as regional centers. The importance of their regional hinterlands and their membership in a regional urban network was most apparent in the economic rivalry that developed among the cities of the Pacific Coast. Even while they were concerned with the national reputations of their cities, the businessmen were also very interested in their regional rankings. To some extent, the intercity rivalry on the Pacific Coast mirrored rivalries that had grown between other groups of cities at earlier dates. Contests among Boston, Philadephia, and New York had enlivened the late eighteenth and early nineteenth centuries.[46] Competition among Cincinnati, Lexington, St. Louis, Louisville, and Pittsburgh spurred the development of the Ohio Valley; and rivalry between St. Louis and Chicago contributed to the growth of the Midwest.[47]

Central to the contest for hegemony over the Pacific Coast were battles to control its economic hinterland, with its rich resources in minerals, lumber, and agricultural products. The struggle for the interior took place in two overlapping stages. As they matured, Portland and Seattle eroded the control that San Francisco once maintained over the Pacific Northwest. Then contests developed at more local levels. Seattle and Portland battled for the Pacific Northwest, while Oakland and Los Angeles challenged San Francisco for dominance within California.[48] San Franciscans were quick to bewail the change. As one merchant lamented in 1893:

Our city is in a state of lethargy and passes her time musing upon the past. . . . A visit to the southern part of the state must necessarily move the mind to a very serious consideration of our present inertia. Los Angeles, in a very homely western phrase that is suggestive, if not altogether true, says that we are "not in it." Today Los Angeles imports directly and is competing with San Francisco in towns as far north as Merced. We have lost very largely our northern trade [to Portland and Seattle], and which country is fast becoming important in its commercial sense. Salt Lake and Ogden can today deal with the East to their advantage, and Mexico is now importing her mining machinery from that district, notwithstanding that our city could supply a superior article.[49]

Until the 1880s, San Franciscans controlled most of the interior of the Pacific Coast as their economic hinterland. Before the coming of the railroad, San Francisco served as the major distributing point for supplies coming around Cape Horn for mining towns throughout the West. Even after the completion of the first transcontinental railroad in 1869, San Francisco retained its dominant position when new mining strikes were made. By a circuitous water route, goods from San Francisco reached parts of eastern Washington, Idaho, and even Montana. In return, many of the products of the mines and farms of the Pacific Coast went east through San Francisco.[50]

However, during the last two decades of the nineteenth century Seattle and Portland merchants took over most of the trade with the interior of the Pacific Northwest. With the completion of the Northern Pacific and Great Northern Railroads, the businessmen of the two cities extended their reach into the countryside; and the economic hinterland of San Francisco merchants correspondingly contracted. Although San Francisco merchants could wistfully consider competing with their northern counterparts for the trade of the Idaho Basin as late as 1912, such hopes had, in fact, proved illusory long before.[51] Indeed, by the first decade of the twentieth century, Portland merchants, blessed by favorable railroad rates, had captured much of the trade of northern California.[52]

As they broke the hold of San Franciscans over the Pacific Northwest, Seattle and Portland business leaders came into conflict with each other. Portland merchants viewed Seattleites as brash upstarts invading what should be their natural trade territory—most of the Pacific Northwest, including eastern Washington. To combat the work of Seattle's businessmen, Portland's merchants mounted one trade excursion after another to try to keep the products of the interior flowing down the Columbia River to their city rather than across the Cascade Mountains by railroad to Seattle. In early May 1909, for example, seventy-five Portland merchants belonging to that city's Commercial Club traveled by train throughout eastern Washington "to advance the interests and influence of Portland throughout the territory."[53] Seattle's merchants countered with their own excursions and in time won much of the trade in agricultural goods that had previously traveled to Portland for processing and shipment to market.

Shortly after they had lost control of the trade of the Pacific Northwest, San Francisco businessmen found themselves seriously challenged within their own state by merchants from Los

Angeles. The contest for the interior of California centered upon the San Joaquin Valley, which became a valuable prize through the development of fruit and vegetable farming and by the discovery of oil there. Los Angeles merchants took advantage of the confusion following the San Francisco earthquake and fire of 1906 to penetrate far north into the valley. San Francisco jobbers soon spotted that threat to their livelihood, and in response petitioned the California Railroad Commission to restructure railroad rates into the valley in a way that would favor them over their southern counterparts.[54] The effort was of no avail. Accepting arguments from Los Angeles businessmen, the commission reduced rates from the southern city into the valley on the grounds that increased traffic justified lower rates. In 1911 the frustrated secretary of San Francisco's Civic League, an organization of the city's leading merchants, sourly described the railroad system of California and much of the West as being "in the form of a large funnel . . . with its spout at Los Angeles."[55]

Closely related to the contests for the interior were struggles to control the coastal commerce and foreign trade of the Pacific Coast. Although by the twentieth century much of the mineral, forest, and agricultural goods going to the Pacific Coast cities stayed in them to be processed and consumed locally, much was also shipped out to other destinations. The imminent completion of the Panama Canal in the early twentieth century added a fillip to the competition in foreign trade.[56] The merchants of all of the Pacific Coast cities expected the opening of the canal to increase their trade greatly. They, however, tempered their optimism with the uneasy realization that they would be in fierce competition with each other for that commerce. By the early twentieth century, Portland and Seattle, supported by their thriving hinterlands, were rivaling San Francisco as seaports. In 1910 the value of foreign trade passing through San Francisco was $87 million, that going through Seattle $66 million.[57] Within California, Oakland and Los Angeles challenged San Francisco for trade. As part of their planning activities, the business groups sponsored a wide range of harbor improvements—new piers, breakwaters, and deepwater channels—and, prodded by shippers, city governments successfully wrested control of their harbors away from railroads, which, the merchants believed, were not doing enough to develop them.

The cities of the Pacific Coast developed primarily as trade centers, but in the twentieth century industry grew in significance; and here, too, intercity rivalry was important. Portland and Seattle came increasingly into conflict with each other for industrial markets. In 1911 and 1912, for example, Portland's manufacturers led a Made in Oregon movement, designed to persuade their state's residents to purchase products put together only in Oregon.[58] In California the rivalry pitted manufacturers in San Francisco, Los Angeles, and Oakland against each other. The earthquake and fire of 1906 slowed San Francisco's industrial advance. Some firms moved to Oakland and Los Angeles, and relatively few new ones located in San Francisco. To reverse that trend, San Francisco industrialists mounted a drive for "home patronage of home industry," but to little effect. Los Angeles, in particular, moved ahead as a center for oil refineries, rubber plants, aviation, and motion pictures, until by 1930 the value of those and other products surpassed that of San Francisco's manufacturers.[59]

It was to remedy the perceived problems and to take advantage of opportunities resulting from rapid economic, population, and spatial growth that some Pacific Coast urbanites, especially some businessmen, turned to civic improvements and city planning. Through planning they hoped to channel economic growth along desired lines and place their cities ahead of their urban rivals. Through planning they sought to win national recognition for their cities as mature members of the nation's expanding urban network. Through planning they sought to create a sense of civic patriotism, thereby healing the population divisions in their urban centers, and through planning they hoped to reunite their spatially dispersed metropolises.

2

San Francisco Rejects the Burnham Plan

▼

At 5:14 A.M. on April 18, 1906, an earthquake less than one minute in duration rumbled through San Francisco, leveling buildings, rupturing gas pipes, and breaking water mains. The earthquake set the stage for disaster. Within just a few hours, local fires resulting from the broken gas pipes and overturned stoves coalesced into a major conflagration that burned unchecked for three days. Mary Austin, who like many others was forced from her home by the fire, vividly recounted the scene a few weeks later:

> Before the red night paled into murky dawn thousands of people were vomited out of the angry throat of the street far down toward Market [Street]. . . . There was a strange, hot, sickish smell in the street as if it had become the hollow slot of some fiery breathing snake. I came out and stood in the pale pinkish glow and saw a man I knew hurrying down toward the gutted district . . . "Bob," I said, "it looks like the day of Judgment!"[1]

The fire destroyed the heart of San Francisco—almost five square miles encompassing the financial district, the major retail district, and much of the wholesale, factory, and entertainment sections of the city. Only the harbor facilities, which could be protected by streams of water from fireboats, survived in the downtown area. Burning an area one and one-half times as large as the great Chicago fire of 1871, the San Francisco fire gutted some 28,000 buildings in 521 blocks. Between 500 and 3,000 people died, and another 250,000, about three-fifths of the population, were left homeless.[2]

Despite its extensive destruction, San Francisco was functioning again within a remarkably short time. (The Golden Gate Tennis Club, although handicapped by courts with cracked baselines, was able to hold a tournament just three weeks after the earthquake.) With immediate recovery under way, San Franciscans faced the larger tasks of reconstruction. How would they rebuild their city? Would they reconstruct San Francisco as the city had existed before the disaster or would they rebuild it along new lines? By the destruction they caused, the earthquake and fire removed one of the main impediments to urban modernization. By destroying old structures, the disaster removed physical limitations on city development. The opportunity to build anew along planned lines was thus most pronounced in San Francisco of all of the Pacific Coast cities. Yet, despite the availability of a city plan that had been drawn up just before the earthquake and fire, San Franciscans rebuilt in a largely unplanned manner, perpetuating many of the problems from which they had long suffered.

Planning Begins in San Francisco

Efforts to improve San Francisco preceded disaster by about a decade, and business organizations led the initial campaigns. Foremost among them was the San Francisco Merchants' Association, established in 1894 by forty-seven leading merchants and bankers. From the first, members equated business development with civic progress. According to its constitution, the organization was set up "to further the best interests of San Francisco and

The 1906 earthquake and fire severely damaged San Francisco's old city hall. From the Burnham Plan for San Francisco.

thereby prove beneficial to the mercantile community." Within four years the body had 1,003 members and was working for better street cleaning, lighting, and paving, the establishment of boulevards, improved fire protection, and a free public market.[3]

Businessmen formed other bodies that also pressed for city betterments. In 1897 the Real Estate Dealers' Association came out for the establishment of a municipally owned water supply.[4] By 1899 San Francisco also possessed at least thirty active neighborhood improvement clubs, composed primarily of local businessmen pledged to improving their city's streets, public buildings, sewers, and water supply.[5] Like members of the Merchants' Association, those belonging to the improvement clubs viewed civic and business progress as identical. As one club member observed, the improvements "will bring an era of prosperity to San Francisco."[6]

Beyond piecemeal improvements for their city, a few San Franciscans were beginning to think in terms of broader planning. By far the most important among these was James Duvall Phelan, Jr. Phelan was a second-generation San Franciscan whose father had come to the city as a forty-niner and had quickly made a fortune in trade, real estate, and banking. Born in 1861 and educated in San Francisco, Phelan inherited and added to the family fortune as a bank president and real estate developer. His interests soon extended beyond business to encompass civic affairs. Phelan served as the vice-president of the California World's Fair Commission in 1893 and managed the state's exhibit in Chicago. Like so many who saw the "White City," with its stately buildings grouped according to an overall plan, Phelan was profoundly moved by the experience. Upon returning to San Francisco, he helped start the Mid-Winter Fair in 1894, a local continuation of the Chicago exposition.[7]

Seeing in politics an arena in which he might leave his imprint upon San Francisco, Phelan won election as the city's mayor in 1896, 1898, and 1899. As mayor, Phelan found himself mixing politics with his desire to improve San Francisco. As a private citizen, Phelan had been the president of the San Francisco Art Association in 1894 and 1895. While he was mayor, that organization petitioned Phelan to appoint a committee to prepare a plan for the "adornment" of San Francisco. Phelan readily complied, setting up a committee of businessmen, lawyers, architects, and artists. Nothing immediately came of the effort, however.[8]

Phelen was more successful in 1898 in winning approval for a new city charter from the electorate. Establishing a new board of supervisors elected at large (the older one had been elected by district), increasing the authority of the mayor, and giving the city the power to purchase utilities from private companies, the charter greatly strengthened the city government. The increase in power, combined with the fact that the city had the authority in most cases to issue its own bonds without prior approval from the state legislature, set the stage for more vigorous actions by city officials. During the next decade and a half, city officials—prodded by businessmen—would use their bonding power to improve San Francisco (the bonds were general obligation bonds requiring a two-thirds favorable vote and paid for primarily by property taxes).[9] By 1915, San Francisco ranked fourth among all of the cities in the United States in terms of per capita revenue receipts and outlays.[10]

Although he was the most prominent individual to become interested in civic improvements for San Francisco, Phelan was not alone. In 1899, for example, B. J. S. Cahill, an English-born architect who had moved to San Francisco and who had submitted a plan for the new University of California campus in Berkeley, put forward a plan for the creation of a civic center in San Francisco. Cahill called for the rerouting of Market Street, the city's main commercial thoroughfare, around an island of three blocks in the downtown area and the siting of public buildings on those blocks. While nothing resulted immediately from Cahill's urgings, they, like Phelan's activities, aroused public interest in civic improvements.[11]

By the late 1890s, San Franciscans were, then, becoming increasingly interested in civic improvements. Merchant groups, real estate bodies, local improvement associations, and some individual businessmen and professionals like Phelan and Cahill were putting forward a growing number of ideas and were becoming involved in the political process. In 1898 the San Francisco *Bulletin* could accurately observe that "there seems to have arisen a general enthusiasm for the beautifying of the city."[12] Whether the general ideas could be translated into concrete proposals capable of winning voter approval would soon be seen. The first test came in the 1899 city election when San Franciscans voted on $10 million in bonds for sewer, school, park, and hospital improvements.

The bonds won strong backing from the Merchants' Association and some thirty of San Francisco's improvement clubs, joined together as the Public Improvement Central Club.[13] Through civic improvements San Francisco could win recognition for itself and, as Andrea Sbarboro, the president of the Italian-American Bank and the head of the Public Improvement Central Club, explained, assume its proper place in the nation's urban network. "It behooves all citizens to advance San Francisco to the place to which her natural advantages entitle her," he argued.[14] Direct economic benefits were possible. "Beautifying a city pays enormous returns on the expenditure . . . [as] demonstrated in the case

35

of Paris," Sbarboro noted. "In our case the proposed park system will enhance real estate values [and] as the years pass and our city is made more attractive, the increase in population and consequent improvements will reduce taxes to a minimum."[15] Then, too, the bonds were needed to allow San Francisco to catch up with Oakland and Los Angeles, cities, Sbarboro observed, that "lead us in schools."[16] The only organized busines opposition came from the San Francisco Real Estate Association, whose members feared higher real estate taxes.

Supporters added that passage of the bonds was needed to create public works jobs for laborers, though there was far from unanimity on that point. P. H. McCarthy, the president of the city's strong Building Trades Council put forward the argument for jobs most forcefully. He was joined by James Phelan, who actively worked for the bonds. Phelan observed that "the carpenter, the brickman, the plumber, the cabinetmaker, tradesman, and laborer will be direct beneficiaries. In the grading, bridge-building, and maintenance of the new grounds, labor will find employment." Nonetheless, the San Francisco Labor Council opposed the bonds as being "for the benefit of the rich" and because "the importation of labor [to work on the city projects] would injure the workingmen already here."[17]

More than economic progress and civic recognition were at stake in the minds of the bond proponents, for a quest for civic unity also inspired them. Nowhere was that clearer than in the many speeches made by Phelan. The heart and soul of the bond campaign, Phelan linked civic patriotism to civic beauty, commerce, and jobs in talk after talk. In a public appeal for bonds to pay for new land for parks and boulevards, Phelan foreshadowed many of the arguments used during the next decade in favor of city planning in San Francisco:

> The people should patriotically arise to the occasion and not thwart a great public work by bickerings or lack of confidence in the future of their city. By making San Francisco beautiful and attractive the outlay will be repaid many times by increasing population, flow of visitors, and a happy contented people. Labor will get employment not only in the public works, but permanently in the demand for work which

comes to great cities when their attractions draw and hold a large number of people.[18]

A broadside distributed by the improvement clubs summarized the diverse social and economic reasons supporters favored the bonds: "Vote for progress and prosperity; vote for the adornment of the city; vote for health and recreation for the people; vote for the employment of labor."[19]

The bonds won approval handily.[20] At that time, most groups could agree that substantial city improvements were needed in San Francisco.[21] Sbarboro spoke for a growing number of businessmen the day after the election when he said that "capitalists will now feel more confident and will invest money in improving the city . . . this will give new life to all industries and permanent employment for many years to come to our laborers."[22] Phelan, always interested in making San Francisco one of America's leading cities, asserted, "By the vote of today we have taken our position confidently among the great cities and the people have shown a spirit that will carry them to success."[23] Phelan and Sbarboro spoke too soon, however. The bonds were nullified on a legal technicality, and only a few improvements took place during the next four years.

Almost the same scenario recurred in 1903, as San Franciscans voted on bonds for hospital, sewer, school, street, library, jail, playground, and park improvements. Many of the same arguments employed in 1899 were used again. Civic pride, a desire to place their city among the first rank of American metropolises, remained very important to the bond supporters. Frank Symes, the president of the San Francisco Merchants Association, decried the state of city services as "humiliating . . . an absolute discredit to any first-class city" and called for the passage of the bonds to rectify the situation.[24] F. W. Dohrman, one of San Francisco's leading merchants, argued in a similar vein that only through the improvements made possible by the bonds could San Francisco "step forward and take its rank and its position among the large cities of the world."[25] Intercity rivalry led some to support the bonds. The head of the California Club noted that Seattle possessed "the most exquisite of Western parks," and called on San Franciscans to vote for the bonds to make their city "ready to meet her great destiny as a queen city."[26]

As in 1899, direct economic benefits were also seen as coming from the bonds by their supporters. Improvement clubs and the Merchants' Association backed the bonds as "a good business proposition" because coordinated improvements would be cheaper than improvements made "piecemeal." Moreover, it was expected that "if we make the city more delightful, more people will come here to live" and that "San Francisco, under such stimulus, will go ahead."[27] McCarthy of the Building Trades Council again favored the bonds as likely to provide employment for construction workers, but he added, too, that "we ought to have a beautiful city in which we can all live and feel proud of it."[28] Phelan, now a private citizen and no longer mayor, campaigned for the bonds. In addition to the arguments he had used in 1899, Phelan added the claim that improvements to San Francisco would make the city more "wholesome," thus encouraging people "to flock here from the suburbs where they now go for health."[29]

Facing no organized opposition, the bonds once more easily won approval. However, when offered for sale in September 1904, the bonds found few takers because the interest rates had been set too low. At that point, a new civic group entered the fray: the Association for the Improvement and Adornment of San Francisco (AIASF), composed mainly of the city's leading merchants. At a meeting with bankers, the association's members convinced San Francisco's financiers to purchase some of the bonds.[30]

Like their counterparts across the United States, San Francisco businessmen employed an organizational approach to problem solving in the opening years of the twentieth century. Intensified labor-management conflict was eroding popular support for business-sponsored urban improvements in San Francisco, causing business leaders, especially merchants, to form their own organization explicitly devoted to bringing about civic improvements. A bitter two-month strike in 1901 pitted the merchants against the city's powerful teamsters and waterfront workers. When Mayor Phelan intervened on behalf of the employers, he began losing labor support for, among other things, his plans for civic improvements. The strike ushered in a decade of conflict between management and labor in San Francisco. As part of the conflict, in 1901 labor leaders organized their own political party, the Union Labor party; and that party succeeded in controlling much of city politics for the next nine years. Eugene Schmitz of the Union

Labor party became mayor; and Abe "Boss" Ruef, the real power in the party, ran city politics. When the Union Labor party proved to be not only unresponsive to their wishes but also corrupt, some of San Francisco's business elite looked for new methods by which to influence their city's development.[31]

Some sought to reform their city's politics, and from this effort may be traced the origins of progressivism in San Francisco and California.[32] Fremont Older, the editor of the *San Francisco Bulletin;* Rudolph Spreckels, whose family had made a small fortune in sugar refining; James Phelan; and other business leaders mounted a campaign to expose corruption in the Union Labor party. In a series of investigations lasting into 1907, they ultimately proved successful. Schmitz was removed from office, and Ruef was sent to the state prison at San Quentin. From 1907 onward the reform movement in San Francisco merged with similar developments elsewhere in California to give rise to the progessive movement in the state.

At the same time that they were beginning to try to change politics in San Francisco, business leaders set up the AIASF in January 1904. A meeting of "about twenty gentlemen" called by Phelan, J. W. Byrne, the president of the Pacific Union Club, and Willis Davis, the president of the San Francisco Art Association, convened in the building of the San Francisco Merchants' Exchange to found the association. The letter of invitation to those founding the organization stated that "The object of the meeting is to formally discuss a plan for the improvement of San Francisco" and noted that "the plan contemplates making San Francisco a more desirable city in which to live."[33] Phelan, who was the most important figure in the formation of the group, appealed to the civic pride of San Franciscans. "San Francisco is at a turning point of its growth," he observed. The city could either become a world leader or fall to second-class status. "It can either be a great and beautiful and attractive city where men and women of civilized tastes and wants will desire to live, or a great and ugly and forbidding city which people will shun."[34]

Composed mainly of members of San Francisco's merchant and banking elite (including the president of the Merchants' Association and the head of the Merchants' Exchange), the AIASF grew rapidly, attaining 377 members within a year.[35] Those joining the AIASF had in mind a multitude of individual civic improvements: the construction of an opera house, auditorium, and music conser-

39

vatory, street and boulevard improvements, the creation of ter-
raced parks, and other projects.[36] From the outset, however, the
AIASF's overriding concern was the preparation of a "comprehensive plan" for San Francisco as a means of achieving an "elevation
of the public taste" and as a "great advertisement for our city."[37]
In an open letter to the general public in late April 1904, the
directors of the AIASF summed up its goals, which, like those of
the Merchants' Association put forward a decade earlier, blended
civic pride, business growth, and urban development:

> The main objects of the Association are to promote in every
> practical way the beautifying of streets, public buildings,
> parks, squares, and places of San Francisco; to bring to the
> attention of the officials and people of the city the best methods
> for instituting artistic municipal improvements; to stimulate
> the sentiment of civic pride in the improvement and care of pri-
> vate property; to suggest quasi-public enterprises and, in short,
> make San Francisco a more agreeable city in which to live.[38]

Elected president of the AIASF, Phelan moved quickly to make
those ideas reality. Even before the association had been founded,
Phelan had sounded out Daniel Burnham, America's best-known
urban planner, about the possibility of coming to San Francisco to
prepare a city plan. Burnham had been in overall charge of de-
signing the architecture of the World's Columbian Exposition in
Chicago in 1893, had headed the commission to draw up a plan for
Washington, D. C., in 1901 and 1902, and had been involved in
planning the layout for new government buildings in Cleveland in
1902 and 1903.[39] In early February 1904, the AIASF extended an
invitation to Burnham.[40]

Burnham accepted with alacrity on the conditions that the
association would pay his expenses and that he would be able to
name his subordinates. Those conditions were met, and Burnham
came to San Francisco in late spring, bringing with him his tal-
ented young assistant Edward Bennett. (This was Bennett's first,
but not his last, experience with western cities. He would go on to
design a city plan for Portland.) Welcoming Burnham to San Francisco at a dinner at the St. Francis Hotel in early May, Phelan
caught the feeling of optimism of the day in observing that "a new

spirit has taken hold of San Francisco to make San Francisco live-
able and loveable—to make it worthy of its position and destiny,"
and the members of the AIASF endorsed a resolution calling upon
Burnham "to draft a plan for the improvement and advancement
of San Francisco."[41]

Burnham and Bennett, assisted by the San Francisco architect
Willis Polk, set up a studio atop the Twin Peaks from which they
could view the city; and from that perch they labored throughout
1904 and 1905 to draft a city plan for San Francisco. Burnham was
away much of the time drawing up plans for a redesigned Manila
and a new summer capital for the Philippines at Baguio. As a consequence, much of the work devolved upon Bennett, Polk, and others.[42] As promised, the AIASF paid for the work, the cost of which
came to sixteen thousand dollars, assisted by large donations from
Phelan, Spreckels, the Southern Pacific Railroad, the United Railroads of San Francisco (the city's private street railroad system), the
San Francisco Lumber Dealers' Exchange, the San Francisco Gas
and Electric Company, the Pacific Mail Steamship Company, the
Brewers' Protective Association, the Emporium (the city's major
department store), and several leading merchants.[43]

The arrival of Burnham spurred the AIASF on to new efforts.
The organization set up an advisory council to meet on a regular
basis with Burnham and his assistants and arranged hearings at
which representatives of business bodies, improvement clubs, and
some labor groups presented ideas as the work progressed. The
AIASF also continued its own efforts to improve San Francisco,
mounting campaigns for the planting of flowers and trees, the extension of parks, the building of better streets, the prohibition of
overhead trolley-car wires on Sutter and Market streets as not befit-
ting "the dignity and beauty of our principal streets," and the construction of harbor improvements made "necessary by the growth
of commerce and the increasing population" of San Francisco.[44]

The Burnham Plan

Completed late in the summer of 1905, the Burnham Plan for
San Francisco set a pattern to be repeated in city plans prepared

throughout America during the Progessive Era in aiming at making radical changes in the physical layout of San Francisco. "We must remember that a meager plan will fall short of perfect achievement, while a great one will yield large results," Burnham trumpeted. While visionary in his scope, Burnham could, nonetheless, be practical in how he thought his plan should be implemented. "It is not to be supposed that all the work indicated can or should be carried out at once," he wrote. Rather, he thought, "a plan beautiful and comprehensive enough for San Francisco can only be executed by degrees."[45]

Influenced by his study of Paris, Berlin, Vienna, Moscow, and London, Burnham thought that a city should be laid out in series of concentric circles, with each circle having a different role in the life of the city. "The city may be divided into the following elements: 1st—Administrative and Educational; 2nd—Economical; 3rd—Residential," Burnham explained. The first "element," that is, the administrative and educational center, would be, he thought, "the real being of the city proper . . . it guarantees the city's relation to the country and its civic character to the citizens."[46] Beyond the first zone would be a second area for business and commercial purposes and a third one for homes.

Replanning San Francisco's street system occupied much of the Burnham Plan, for Burnham believed that wide streets circling cities should clearly delineate the various zones of activity in them. Joining the concentric streets would be arterials slicing diagonally through the city. In putting his ideas into practice in San Francisco, Burnham had to modify them to take account of the city's hilly topography. No single web of concentric streets and arterials was possible. Instead, Burnham proposed multiple sets of street webs radiating outward from a number of centers within San Francisco. Only two streets, a Perimeter of Distribution and an Outer Boulevard, completely circled San Francisco in Burnham's plan. Beyond those grand designs, numerous proposals to relocate individual streets were laid out in the Burnham Plan. Burnham thus sought to modify greatly San Francisco's existing gridiron street plan.[47]

Burnham also called for the construction of a civic center composed of governmental and educational buildings arranged in such a way as to contribute to "public rest and recreation and adapted to celebrations, fetes, etc."[48] Cahill, the architect who

Daniel Burnham's proposed civic center, viewed from the south side of Market Street. From the Burnham Plan for San Francisco.

had drafted a plan for a civic center in 1899, anticipated the inclusion of a civic center in the Burnham Plan. He reworked his plan, moving the civic center off Market Street to a plaza to the west, and presented it to Burnham and Bennett for their consideration. Burnham and Bennett, however, rejected Cahill's proposal, favoring a civic center consisting of a ring of buildings located at the intersection of Market Street and Van Ness Avenue a number of blocks south of the major downtown area.[49] At various points throughout the city there would also be smaller public "places" removed "from the direct flow and press of business" and designed "to strengthen the public sense of the dignity and responsibility of citizenship."[50]

Parks and boulevards attracted Burnham's attention, as they

did that of most city planners in the Progressive Era. Burnham suggested the creation of large parks, smaller playgrounds, and parkways throughout San Francisco. They would, he argued, serve the practical purpose of acting as "an effective barrier" to the spread of fires. Moreover, parks would, he believed, instill desirable moral values in those who frequented them. In calling for a formal layout in the parks, Burnham noted that "in the smaller parks this amounts to a lesson of order and system, and its influence on the masses cannot be overestimated." Similarly, he hoped that public meetings in playgrounds would "replace the old neighborhood stagnation with . . . unity of purpose and development."[51] Burnham shared the belief common in the Progressive period that the character of people could be altered by changing the environments within which they lived. Parks could be a major tool in that process.

Burnham envisaged the development of an orderly San Francisco united by a sense of civic patriotism, a city whose different parts and people would all function together harmoniously. While a major advance in city planning for its day and while addressing real problems San Franciscans faced, the Burnham Plan, nonetheless, left much unsaid. Although recognizing that a city was composed of different "elements," Burnham spent most of his plan discussing streets and parks. While some of San Franscico's merchants were beginning to worry about the erosion of their city's hegemony over the Pacific Coast, the Burnham Plan did not adequately address their concerns. Housing, the harbor, and the economy of San Francisco received scant attention. Like most city beautiful plans of the Progressive Era, the Burnham Plan dealt incompletely with the economic life of the metropolis for which it was designed. Those deficiencies, while not fully recognized in 1905, would cause problems for planning proponents later on.

San Francisco and the Origins of City Beautiful

With the preparation of the Burnham Plan, San Franciscans, despite the plan's shortcomings, assumed a position of leadership in the city planning movement emerging in early twentieth-century America. Americans generally were rediscovering the city and across much of the nation were reacting to the problems they found by advocating city planning. Like most Americans of the Progressive Era, those involved in the planning movement were optimistic about the future of cities.

The nascent planning movement had diverse roots. Some planning proponents took their inspiration from Chicago's Columbian Exposition of 1893 and the replanning of Washington, D.C., about a decade later. Burnham and Phelan clearly fit into that group. Others came to support planning as a result of their work as city engineers laying out street and sewer systems. While that approach to planning would be important in some other Pacific Coast cities—Seattle, for example—it was of less significance in San Francisco. Still other planning advocates began their efforts in local grass roots projects involving neighborhood improvement associations pushing for municipal art, civic improvements of various sorts, and outdoor art. That approach to planning was of considerable significance in San Francisco, as revealed in the 1899 and 1903 bond campaigns.[52]

Urban improvements were not new to America in the Progressive Era. From the time of the building of the first North American cities in the colonial period, some people had worked to make their urban environments better places in which to live. Parks, boulevards, civic buildings and so on had all been parts of those early improvement efforts.[53] What was new, at least for most of those involved in the Progressive-Era planning movements, was what they viewed as *comprehensive* planning: the notion that all of the various individual aspects of improvements should be coordinated to reinforce each other. Planning proponents came increasingly to think that cities should be developed along lines laid down by overall city plans. As the historian William Wilson has observed in his study of the city beautiful movement in five cities across America, "Its development of the comprehensive plan marked the City Beautiful era's great departure from the past."[54] As in the case of San Francisco, however, those plans rarely considered all of the needs of the residents of America's cities. Too often the plans were concerned too much with the sticks and stones of planning, the needs of the cities, and not enough with the social needs of their citizens. As Wilson has noted, "housing

45

details were outside of the purview of the comprehensive planning of the era."[55]

San Francisco businessmen, like their counterparts elsewhere, were generally optimistic about the prospect of remaking their city. They sensed that man could control his environment, that almost anything could be accomplished. A beautiful planned city would, they thought, lessen discord among different groups and help their cities capture the national reknown they deserved. There was as well a more pessimistic underside to the feelings of San Franciscans, especially some merchants, about their city's destiny. Observing the rise of other Pacific Coast metropolises, they feared for their city's future and saw in planning a way to keep their city abreast of developments occurring elsewhere on the Pacific Coast. A relatively minor note in 1905, their concern would swell to become a mighty chorus as time progressed.

Reconstruction and City Planning

Calling Burnham's work "complete and satisfactory," the AIASF presented the Burnham Plan to the city government in September 1905 and sought immediate actions on park extensions, the construction of a boulevard around San Francisco, and changes in Market Street. Accepting the plan on behalf of the city, Mayor Schmitz said that the plans gave him "the greatest pleasure" and that he believed in "beginning the work as soon as possible." The Board of Supervisors soon had the Burnham Plan printed as a public document and in mid-April copies were delivered to city hall. By the time of the earthquake and fire, Burnham's ideas were well known. City newspapers had published numerous accounts of his plans for San Francisco, and a display to publicize the plan had been mounted at city hall.[56]

Divisions already existed, however, that would hinder the implementation of the plan. The rift between labor and management, widened by the 1901 strike and subsequent events, continued to grow. The division manifested itself in politics. By this time the graft trials of Schmitz and Ruef were about to begin. Businessmen like Phelan and Spreckels, who were becoming deeply involved in the collection of evidence and legal prosecution of the leaders of the Union Labor party, were unwilling to entrust the planning of their city to the politicians in power.

At this point—in mid-April 1906—the earthquake and fire destroyed much of San Francisco. Far from ending discussion on the Burnham Plan and the future development of San Francisco, the disaster heightened it. Building on their previous experiences, some San Franciscans called for intensified improvement efforts. The Burnham Plan and the future of San Francisco were much in the news in the months following the fire and earthquake.

In the immediate aftermath of the disaster, many San Franciscans were brimming with confidence that their city could be rebuilt along the lines of the Burnham Plan.[57] "Do away with all square blocks and stiff straight lines, and adopt curves, the lines of beauty," the superintendent of the Mountain View Cemetery wrote Phelan one week after the fire had died. "Now at the birth of the city it can be done."[58] Charles Lathrop, the rector of the Church of the Advent and a planning advocate, similarly wrote Phelan a few days later that he hoped the Burnham Plan would be followed in the "marvelous and unique opportunity" to rebuild in a way to ensure not only "the enriching of this city" but also "the bringing up of future generations with blue sky and fields and out of doors to keep people healthy and normal in their ideals."[59]

Organizations responded optimistically to the challenge of rebuilding, capturing in the proclamations of their members some of the same connections between civic pride and economic growth that had characterized the statements of bond supporters in 1899 and 1903. On May 4, the San Francisco Real Estate Board passed a resolution predicting that San Francisco would rise from her ashes "greater, more beautiful and more prosperous," well able "to take a still higher rank among the great cities of the world."[60] The president of the San Francisco Merchants' Exchange made the same point, asserting that "a city is more than a mere collection of houses and humanity. It is an organism . . . [that] can not be destroyed by the mere destruction of part of its physical environment."[61] Similarly, the Outdoor Art League stressed the motto "San Francisco—today in ashes, tomorrow the city beautiful. Watch her grow."[62]

Phelan, who remained at the center of San Francisco's planning movement, was initially confident about his city's future. "San

Francisco's calamity will enable us now to proceed to rebuild the city on the lines of the Burnham Plan," he wrote on April 30, and in early May he could still predict that "the new San Francisco will be finer and greater in every respect." By July, however, Phelan was becoming uncertain about how San Francisco would be rebuilt. "Of course there is sentiment here that resumption of business is the first consideration and an indisposition to make changes that will cost money," he observed in a letter to Andrew Crawford of the American Civic Association.[63] As the course of events would soon show, Phelan's growing reservations were well deserved.

Even as the fire raged across San Francisco, relief activities began. On the afternoon of April 18, Mayor Schmitz convened the Citizens' Committee of Fifty, composed mainly of San Francisco's business leaders, to provide food, clothing, and shelter for the homeless. Phelan headed the subcommittee on finance. The work of the committee was effective, and San Francisco, with its business and political leadership intact, avoided the social disruption that has sometimes characterized cities after disasters.[64]

In early May, a new group—the Committee of Forty, also called the Committee of Reconstruction—replaced the Committee of Fifty. The Committee of Reconstruction was to draft a plan for the rebuilding of San Francisco and report it to the city's Board of Supervisors for implementation. Although composed mainly of business leaders and professionals, the Committee of Reconstruction also included the presidents of the San Francisco Labor Council, the Building Trades Council, and the Carpenters' Union. Phelan chaired two subcommittees, that on boulevards and general beautification (on which he was joined by Spreckels) and that on the Burnham Plan. San Franciscans thus looked beyond their formal system of government for plans and ideas to rebuild their city. An informal government by committee developed to plan for the future of San Francisco.[65]

Optimism initially prevailed in the meetings of the Committee on Reconstruction and its subcommittees. A feeling existed that through planned reconstruction San Francisco could retain, and perhaps even bolster, its position on the Pacific Coast and in the United States. The chairman of the subcommittee on street widening claimed on May 9 that "San Francisco now resembles Paris more than any city in the world," and observed that "ours now are like the chances of youth, which never come again."[66]

Three weeks later, at a joint meeting of the subcommittee on streets with that on the Burnham Plan, the head of the University of California declared that San Francisco was destined to become "vastly bigger and better than ever before." Nevertheless, he warned that "to inspire the confidence of the world and the large financial interests that are expected to play an important part in the upbuilding of the city there should be no deferring of the broad plan."[67]

Acrimony soon crept into the committee deliberations, however, as conflict separated those favoring rapid rebuilding with a minimum of planning as the best way to get San Francisco back on its feet from those desiring more comprehensive planning as better for San Francisco in the long run, even if that meant slowing the process of reconstruction a bit. An editorial in the *Architectural Record*, a national journal, summarized the difficult choice facing San Franciscans. "The conflagration, deplorable as it was, offers San Franciscans a chance to improve the lay out of the city at a much smaller expense than would formerly have been required," observed the editor. The editorial concluded that planned rebuilding might be difficult, however, because "it is possible that the city may not be able to afford such expenditures just now and that it will have to be rebuilt along the old lines."[68] The issue found businessmen on both sides of the matter. Three specific disputes were especially divisive.

Street reconstruction proved to be a particularly contentious issue, for until the locations of streets were fixed and the streets rebuilt, businesses could not fully resume operations. Merchants and other businessmen who had long supported planning now broke from it in the interest of getting back in business as soon as possible. At one point, for instance, the president of the Merchants' Association, who was also a member of the AIASF (which continued to support comprehensive planning), petitioned the subcommittee on finance to speed up approval for street rebuilding in the downtown area, even if that meant proceeding in a makeshift manner.[69]

Another divisive matter was the proposed extension of new, strict ordinances governing the building of fireproof structures in the downtown district to new areas in an attempt to make San Francisco more secure against future blazes. The attempt led to vociferous opposition from small-business owners outside the downtown fire limits as too expensive and as "a land-grabbing scheme on the part of the big capitalists." It would be better to have "a city that might burn than no city at all," argued one small retailer worried about the cost of rebuilding.[70]

A third issue that immediately surfaced was that of the building of a civic center. Just one week after the earthquake and fire, Phelan issued a call to "all interested architects, engineers, and others" to come together to discuss the rebuilding of the city at a meeting of the AIASF. In May the association resolved that a new civic center should be constructed at Market and Van Ness, as specified in the Burnham Plan, and urged the Board of Supervisors to purchase the necessary four and one-half blocks there. Some businessmen countered, however, that San Francisco could not afford the expense of such a luxury at that time.[71]

Overarching all of those individual issues was, as the editor of the *Architectural Record* foresaw, a common fear on the part of many businessmen that with their property destroyed they could not afford the higher taxes they thought would be required by the improvements mandated by planning. An editorial in the San Francisco *Chronicle* three weeks after the earthquake caught that feeling well:

> Every individual in the city is practicing economy. So must the city itself. . . . Capital will not come here either on loan or for purchase if confronted with the prospect of excessive taxation. There must be the strictest economy in government. There must be the strictest economy in improvements. We all desire the city beautiful just as we desire the home beautiful, but the business man who at this juncture should attempt to borrow money to decorate his home would knock in vain at the doors of any bank in America.[72]

Politics further muddied the waters, making agreements on rebuilding still more difficult. By 1906 and 1907, graft prosecutions of Union Labor party leaders were under way.[73] Even as the prosecutions were first contemplated and then begun, the boss of the party, Abe Ruef, sought to take advantage of San Francisco's disaster by enriching himself through real estate dealings involving political manipulations. Ruef's actions further widened the gap between business and labor and made business leaders still more reluctant to entrust the rebuilding of their city to the politicians in power. In late 1906 and early 1907, the Merchants' Association, which continued to back rebuilding along the lines of the Burnham Plan, called for a "thorough moral regeneration" of San Francisco's politics and attacked grafters as "traitors" to their city.[74] By the spring of 1907, the organization's president was at one and the same time calling for the creation of "the San Francisco Beautiful," praising Spreckels for his work in fighting graft, and noting that in times gone past corrupt politicians were "instantly shot."[75]

With San Francisco's business leaders divided and with rifts between labor leaders and businessmen widening, the concept of comprehensive, coordinated planning was lost in the reality of piecemeal rebuilding. The Committee on Reconstruction recommended numerous individual street, park, and building improvements to the city government, and many of them were adopted. However, no real effort was made to follow the Burnham Plan in the reconstruction of San Francisco. Summoned back to San Francisco to offer advice on reconstruction, Burnham lamented at one point that the report of the Committee on Reconstruction had nothing to do with his plan but was designed simply to relieve the congestion of the downtown area.[76] The plan could have been followed. Through newspaper coverage it was well known by this time, and it was detailed enough in its recommendations to have provided close guidance in the reconstruction of the city.

Particularly disappointing to planning proponents was a failure to rebuild the industrial and commercial area south of Market Street along new lines suggested by Marsden Manson, a former city engineer, in a detailed report submitted to the Committee on Reconstruction in September 1906. Calling for new street layouts, better fire-fighting facilities, and the regrading of hills, the report would have adapted the Burnham Plan to a major renovation of the South of Market District. "Five or ten years from now it will be absolutely impossible to make these improvements," Manson argued. "They must be made now or they will never be made. . . . I earnestly recommend these improvements so that San Francisco may at least stand ready to hold her commercial supremacy on the Pacific Coast."[77] Nonetheless, in their haste to rebuild, San Franciscans largely ignored his report.

While eliminating physical limitations on urban development,

51

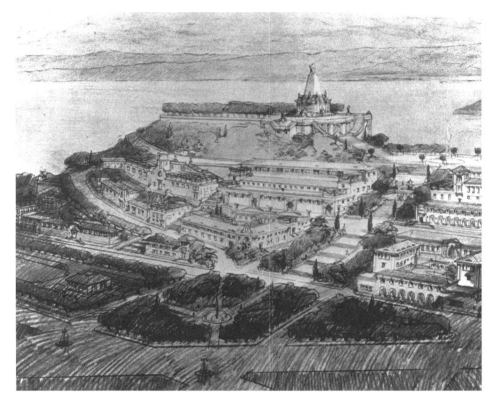

Daniel Burnham proposed terracing Telegraph Hill. From the Burnham Plan for San Francisco.

the earthquake and fire left political and social impediments intact. Although not apparent in the first burst of relief and recovery activities, political and social divisions surfaced when San Franciscans turned to the issue of long-range reconstruction. Divisions separating different groups within San Francisco made comprehensive planning impossible to achieve. As Thomas Maggee, the head of the Merchants' Association and a strong supporter of the Burnham Plan, lamented, "Men are mostly moved by selfish interests. . . . I thought after the fire that at last San Francisco was going to pull together. For a few weeks it appeared that way, but I must confess that today we seem to be splitting apart wider than ever. What is going to pull us together?"[78]

Private and Public Planning,

1907–1912

Nonetheless, a desire for urban improvements persisted. Throughout 1907 and 1908, San Franciscans labored through a growing number of neighborhood improvement associations for street improvements, better lighting, and the creation of neighborhood parks—all deemed necessary for comfortable urban life, and all seen as needed to stay abreast of what other Pacific Coast cities were doing.[79] Moreover, San Franciscans supported what they viewed as essential, practical citywide services. They hesitated, however, at more grandiose proposals and never returned fully to the idea of comprehensive planning embodied in the Burnham Plan.

In 1908 San Franciscans approved $18 million worth of bonds for their water supply, sewer system, hospitals, hall of justice and jail, schools, and garbage collection system. Solidly supported by the Chamber of Commerce, the Merchants' Association, and the Board of Trade, the bonds won the backing of San Francisco's business and political leaders (by this time the Union Labor party and Mayor Schmitz were being ousted from power) as a matter of civic pride. "It comes down to a question of whether San Francisco shall admit its impotence or whether it shall rise and be the great city it can," observed one supporter.[80] The San Francisco *Chronicle* editorialized in a similar fashion. "Shall this city become known as utterly incorrigible?" the paper asked. "Is there nothing on earth on which its inhabitants can agree?"[81] The bond issue received a mixed reception from labor groups, some of whose members feared higher taxes. While the District Council of Carpenters backed them, the Labor Council, divided, took no official stand, and the Building Trades Council opposed them. Like the bond issues of five years before, the 1908 measures passed by overwhelming majorities in all parts of San Francisco.[82]

Despite the bond victories, San Franciscans continued to oppose matters they deemed less crucial to their city's reconstruction, as revealed in a contest over bonds to build a new civic center a year later. San Francisco's city hall had been heavily damaged by the earthquake and fire and was unusable. The city razed the structure and in 1909 proposed replacing it with a new city hall sited as specified in the Burnham Plan at Market and Van Ness. Buildings to be put up later—a library, public auditorium, and others—would complete the civic center. An $8.48 million bond issue was to pay for the city hall-civic center complex.[83]

Proponents of planning viewed the bond issue as a chance to rescue part of the Burnham Plan. Groups long supporting planning, such as the Merchants' Association and the AIASF, campaigned strongly for the bonds. They were joined by newer city-wide bodies like the San Francisco Art Institute and by business groups that stood to gain the most, such as the Down Town Association and the Mission Promotion Association.[84] Those favoring the bonds discerned a positive link between art and commerce. They saw in a beautiful planned city a way to put San Francisco ahead of its urban rivals, and they viewed passage of the bonds as a way to win national recognition for their city. Phelan, still active in civic affairs, called the bonds a "necessity," if San Francisco was to be a leading American metropolis; and a pamphlet issued by the AIASF claimed that a well-constructed city hall would serve as a model to "encourage private enterprise and give employment to our people."[85] Temporarily called back to San Francisco by the AIASF to work for the bonds, Burnham argued that the civic center would "attract attention to San Francisco from all corners of the globe." Moreover, it would "make of itself a magnet attracting from every quarter those men and fortunes which bring lasting prosperity to a great commercial center."[86] Willis Polk, the San Francisco architect who had assisted Burnham and Bennett and who was a leading member of the AIASF, may have best explained what the bonds meant to their supporters when he spoke to an appreciative audience at a meeting of the Merchants' Association:

> In the days of Pericles, when Athens was at the zenith of her commercial prosperity and had just commenced to feel the rivalry and competition of Syracuse, Pericles cast about for some method by which Athens could retain her commercial supremacy. Finally, merely as a matter of statesmanship, they decided to make Athens beautiful; not for any inherent love of beauty itself, but purely and simply as a business

proposition. . . . If Pericles as a matter of statesmanship did what he did for Athens, don't you think it is up to San Francisco to develop a little statesmanship?[87]

Despite such appeals, opposition quickly developed to the bonds. Many San Franciscans agreed with a speaker addressing the Commonwealth Club, a body composed of businessmen and professionals, who noted that voters had approved $18 million in bonds the year before and therefore could not afford the "frillery and frumpery" of a new city hall.[88] Moreover, as San Francisco recovered from the earthquake and fire and began expanding outward again, numerous local improvement clubs representing suburban neighborhoods opposed the bonds because their members, mainly businessmen, could see no immediate benefits flowing to their localities from the building of the city hall. They were more interested in the extension of city services—water, sewers, police and fire protection—into their neighborhoods. "Why should our taxes be increased for a civic center we don't want when the city has no money to help us out in this district?" asked the president of the Bay View and Visitacion Valley Improvement Club.[89] "When we have no bread," wondered the head of another neighborhood association, "why should we go into debt for pie?"[90]

Faced with widespread opposition, the bonds failed to win approval. Although a majority of voters—12,804 to 10,504—favored them, the bonds fell short of the necessary two-thirds majority. It was the strongly negative votes of the city's outlying suburban residence districts that killed the issue.[91]

With the failure of the city hall-civic center bonds, improvement and planning efforts temporarily shifted to small-scale private projects. For those who could afford to live in them, beautifully laid-out suburbs influenced by British garden city work— Miguel Rancho, Ingleside, and St. Francis Wood—beckoned. Urban rivalry played a role in the planning of those divisions. "San Francisco's outlying residence districts," noted the newsletter of the Merchants' Association in 1911, should be designed to have "the winsome beauty and strong attractiveness of suburbs across the bay and the towns of Southern California."[92] Using both private covenants and city ordinances, real estate community builders sought to create planned enclaves within or just outside of San

Francisco. Similarly, neighborhood improvement efforts in such realms as street lighting and street repairs continued.[93]

From their neighborhood efforts, San Franciscans soon found themselves returning to citywide projects. Preparations for the growth expected to occur in their city with the opening of the Panama Canal, readying their city for visitors attending the Panama–Pacific International Exposition, and changes in city politics all lured San Franciscans to once again enter the realm of citywide planning. This return was, nonetheless, less concerned with comprehensive planning than the campaign for the Burnham Plan had been. Although calling for improvements throughout all of San Francisco, it was more limited in the scope and range of its proposals than had been the Burnham Plan. Ultimately, the new campaign came to focus mainly on building a new civic center and on cleaning up San Francisco for the world's fair. Largely gone was the idea of the coordinated construction of a civic center, parks, boulevards, and streets.

The coming completion of the Panama Canal spurred San Franciscans to reconsider the need for civic improvements. Businessmen in particular wanted to be ready to benefit from what they thought would be a tremendous increase in trade, business, and immigration and were eager to make urban improvements. Merchants, especially, viewed the canal as their salvation in the growing commercial rivalry their city was encountering from other Pacific Coast metropolises. They never tired of pointing out that their community lay astride the shortest circle route through the canal to the Orient and fervently believed that the canal would secure "the permanent installation of San Francisco as a great center of world commerce on the Pacific Ocean."[94]

Business and political leaders realized, however, that the canal would not automatically benefit their city, for other Pacific Coast cities were also getting ready for its opening. As one merchant warned, "Portland, like Seattle, is thoroughly awake to the possibilities of a tremendous increase in business and population following the completion of the Panama canal and is bending every energy in preparing herself for that event. . . . Portland may well be classed as a rival of San Francisco."[95] The message was clear: San Franciscans must also take steps to prepare their city for future growth. One of the city supervisors made that point at the dinner at which a new Chamber of Commerce was formed (in late 1911 the Chamber absorbed the Merchants' Exchange, the Merchants' Association, and the Down Town Association). Noting that the canal would increase trade and manufacturing in San Francisco, he observed that those benefits would materialize only if the city's residents got ready for them through city planning. "Broader streets and brighter parks, a great civic center . . . a new city hall" were needed, he exhorted. Moreover, he thought, "Our hills must be tunnelled to open up new districts to the home seeker."[96] The president of the Chamber of Commerce made many of the same points in his inaugural address in early 1913. Referring to the completion of the canal, he observed that "no American city has ever confronted a period like this. What these years will bring forth depends upon what we do now." He then proceeded to urge chamber members to support city improvements of all types.[97]

The most immediate result of this concern was the boring of a tunnel through the Twin Peaks to open a vast new area to residential development in western San Francisco. The Merchants' Association and some fifty local improvement clubs pushed for the tunnel as a way to prepare their city for "the floodgates of prosperity" they expected to materialize with the opening of the Panama Canal. Unless the tunnel were built, an officer of the Merchant's Association warned, San Francisco would be "outstripped by the smaller cities of the coast."[98] Civic pride was involved. As one San Francisco newspaper observed, "When Seattle finds a hill in her way, she washes it down. Under the same conditions Los Angeles tunnels the hills. . . . What are the people of the earth going to think of us, when they come trooping through the Panama Canal?" He concluded, "We'd better go about a little, take a few lessons in civic pride and patriotism from our sister cities on the coast and then get busy."[99] Only then could San Francisco remain a leading city on the Pacific Coast and in the nation. The city government approved the project in 1912, and work on it began two years later.

The second event igniting interest in citywide improvements was the Panama–Pacific International Exposition. In 1911 San Francisco defeated New Orleans for the right to sponsor this world's fair, due to open its doors in 1915. San Francisco's business leaders quickly came to see the exposition as a chance to show the world how fully their city had recovered from the earthquake and fire. The exposition would, they thought, place their city back on the map. There had already been two forerunners to this exposition. The Portola Festival of 1909 attracted 300,000 visitors to San Francisco and, according to the Merchants' Association, gave the city "the greatest 'ad' it has ever enjoyed."[100] Four years later, the Balboan Exposition provided a further boost.

Even greater results were expected from the Panama–Pacific International Exposition. Warren Manley of the Chamber of Commerce praised it as "a golden opportunity . . . that will undoubtedly never occur again."[101] A desire for civic unity, as well as material progress, motivated some working for the exposition. As early as 1910, the house organ of the Merchants' Association editorialized with approval about preparations for the world's fair, "If eloquence can bury the hatchet, that overworked implement of civic strife and faction is by this time rusting to uselesness in its unmarked grave."[102] Nonetheless, as in the case of the Panama Canal, it was recognized that public improvements would have to be made to prepare their city for the fair. As the head of the San Francisco Real Estate Board explained in late 1911, "The eyes of the world are now and will for the next several years be upon San Francisco. Prospective real estate investors the world over are looking toward San Francisco and California for investment. . . . Let us prepare for our guests by cleaning house."[103] Or, as another San Franciscan noted, "We have invited the world here for 1915. . . . They must not make their way through streets like those of some smoky factory town."[104]

The third change was political. In the 1911 city elections, the Union Labor party was thoroughly ousted from office when James "Sunny Jim" Rolph won the first of five terms as mayor. A banker and shipowner who, nonetheless, had the respect and support of many of San Francisco's workers, Rolph campaigned as a "mayor of all the people, employee as well as employer" and called upon San Franciscans to rise above factionalism. As mayor, he worked hard to unite his city's different groups and restore public confidence in city government. His administration did much to heal the political divisions in San Francisco and thus helped create a political environment within which some city planning efforts could be revived.[105]

Lending structure to the renewed citywide planning campaign was the Civic League of Improvement Clubs. Formed one month after the earthquake and fire to help with the tasks of immediate recovery, the Civic League soon broadened its work. By 1911 the Civic League was composed of delegates from sixty-seven improvement clubs boasting an aggregate membership of eight thousand. The organization hoped to create "a new, clean city, business prosperity, industrial peace, increased commerce, and a pull together to build up San Francisco."[106]

The City Beautiful, the Civic Center, and the Exposition

In 1912 the Civic League led a campaign to beautify San Francisco by dividing the city into twelve districts and presenting prizes to the areas that sponsored the most improvements. Beauty and profits, it was thought, could and should coexist in this campaign. As L. C. Mullgardt, an architect working on the exposition, explained to members of the Down Town Committee of the Chamber of Commerce: "As to the commercial value of beauty, we can not overestimate its vital importance. . . . Numberless American citizens annually flood Asiatic and European towns with their dollars in search for the beautiful. . . . A pecuniary reason is always a good one for doing commendable things."[107] Supported by the new Chamber of Commerce and the Labor Council, the Civic League brought the campaign to a climax with a May Day parade of school children carrying flowers through San Francisco. Once again civic pride, a desire that their city win recognition as a part of the nation's and the world's urban network, motivated San Franciscans. At the conclusion of the parade, Mayor Rolph caught the mood of many when he asserted that San Francisco "will be to America what Florence is to Italy and Paris is to France." He urged his listeners to make San Francisco "the real Exposition City, the City Beautiful."[108]

In 1912, too, San Franciscans reversed their stance of just three years before and approved $8.8 million in bonds to construct a new civic center. To be located at the site of the old city hall, not at the site recommended in the Burnham Plan, the civic center had come to be seen in a new way by most San Franciscans. What they

59

had viewed as a luxury they could not afford in 1909 they now saw as a necessity to prepare their city for the exposition and the canal. "In view of the era of tremendous constructive development before San Francisco," Mayor Rolph told a meeting of neighborhood improvement clubs, "it will be nothing less than a calamity if these bonds are defeated."[109] Civic pride also dictated support for the bonds. Noting that Denver, St. Paul, and Kansas City had recently constructed civic auditoriums, Rolph urged passage for the bonds to allow San Francisco to do the same.[110] Luisa Tetrazzini, the famous opera singer, echoed the mayor, "Other cities, not as large as 'my' city, have it [a civic auditorium] already. Why not here?"[111]

Endorsed by both the Chamber of Commerce and the Labor Council, the civic center bonds faced no organized opposition. With their city well along the road to reconstruction and with city services to the suburbs greatly improved, even most neighborhood improvement clubs, now united in the Civic League, came out for the bonds. The bonds won approval by a margin of ten to one, and construction quickly began on the first buildings of the center. By the time the exposition opened, the city hall and an auditorium had been completed.[112]

Finally, the Panama–Pacific International Exposition, transitory though it was, came to be seen as a climax of the pre–World War I planning movement in San Francisco. Composed of romantically colored buildings grouped together at a waterfront location (what is now the Marina in San Francisco), the exposition, like Chicago's "White City" of twenty-two years before, was an inspiration for the future for many. As one San Franciscan observed, "The Exposition in its ground plan, in its architecture, in its coloring and in its sculpture is the accomplishment of a Utopian ideal in city planning."[113] After visiting the exposition, Burnham was struck by how the fair might reinvigorate the city planning movement in San Francisco. He wrote, "If the Herculean task of developing an Exposition of such classic grandeur, will forever prove an incentive for a more harmonious expansion of our city, San Francisco's millions will have been well spent."[114]

Many business leaders expected the exposition to bring prosperity to their city. They hoped it would win recognition for their city throughout the United States and place it ahead of its urban rivals. The manager of the Bank of California, headquartered in

San Francisco, spoke for many of his colleagues when he predicted that the exposition "will give many businessmen, who have had a hard struggle since the fire a chance to get squarely on their feet again and look the world in the face with considerable cheerfulness."[115] The vice-president of the Chamber of Commerce expanded on this theme when addressing a crowd at the exposition's Chamber of Commerce Day. The exposition would, he thought, "call the attention of the world to this powerful western empire and its chief city and glorious harbor."[116]

More was involved in the exposition, however, than materialistic aspirations. Harkening back to what they incorrectly imagined to have been a time of social unity in the immediate aftermath of the earthquake and fire, some San Franciscans thought they discerned a moral value in the world's fair. They hoped that the fair would unify their city's discordant population. One wrote that "another noticeable phase of the Exposition crowd is a return of that spirit of camaraderie which was peculiar to San Francisco directly after the big fire of 1906. That was a time when social barriers were leveled, an interval of pure democracy."[117] Another warned that "personal ambitions, personal gain, the glorification of the individual must come second to the welfare of the whole . . . commercialism, as merely the glorification of the dollar, must not be allowed to gain a foothold."[118] Some members of the Chamber of Commerce were caught up in that feeling. Exhorting San Franciscans to join in an opening-day parade, the organization's newsletter observed, "Everybody will march. There will be no horses, automobiles, floats, fancy dress, uniforms, or display of any kind." The bulletin went on to claim that "it is the duty of every citizen and businessman to join in this wondrous demonstration. The very future of the city depends upon the success of this undertaking."[119]

Some San Franciscans, especially businessmen, thought they could renew the city's leading role in the economic development of the Pacific Coast through planning. Likewise, they hoped in a more general sense to reassert their city's place in America's urban network.

Such expectations were only partially filled. San Franciscans did achieve some of the separate elements of city planning. New parks and boulevards were established, and beginnings were made on the building of a civic center. With the civic center San

61

Franciscans came, in the words of the scholar Joan Draper, as "as close as almost anybody to realizing the dream of the City Beautiful."[120] Nonetheless, comprehensive planning was not realized. In their haste to rebuild, San Franciscans reconstructed their city in an uncoordinated manner. The social unity sought for by the city's business leaders proved elusive, as renewed group conflicts were to show in the war years and later. Nor were the economic goals fully realized. With the maturation of Los Angeles, Oakland, Seattle, and Portland, San Francisco's dominance over the economy of the Pacific Coast was forever ended.

Beyond the civic center and some park and boulevard improvements, San Franciscans gained little of tangible value from their first efforts at planning. They continued to reject major changes in the layout of their city. In 1913 the consulting engineer Bion Arnold drafted a new plan for the improvement of streets and transportation facilities in San Francisco, but, like the plan drafted by Manson seven years before, it failed to win acceptance. Once again, divisions among different groups hindered its implementation. While parts of the plan were adopted, much of it was ignored.[121] Thus, by the time of the First World War, many proponents of planning believed that they had missed a golden opportunity to rebuild in a comprehensive way after the fire and earthquake. The Burnham Plan had been abandoned. "We used to hear a great deal about the 'City Beautiful' and the opportunity we have for municipal adornment," mused the publication of the Civic League in 1915, "but somehow the city planning pendulum seems to have swung the other way."[122]

3

City Planning in Oakland and Los Angeles

▼

Influenced by the planning efforts in San Francisco, but affected even more by local developments, the residents of Oakland and Los Angeles participated in city planning campaigns. As in San Francisco, the planning movements had diverse origins; but businessmen again played central roles. Business organizations were very active in promoting improvements, and businessmen composed the bulk of the membership in various civic improvement bodies in both cities. Businessmen were not alone in sponsoring the planning campaigns. Charles Mumford Robinson, a well-known eastern planning advocate, prepared a city plan for Oakland in 1906 and a similar one for Los Angeles a year later. City planning in those cities involved more than the Robinson plans, however. In Los Angeles in particular planning assumed varied forms, including one of the pioneering efforts at citywide zoning in the United States.

The Origins of Planning in Oakland

The most powerful initial impetus for the planning movement in Oakland lay in a desire by business leaders to maintain their city's attractiveness as a bedroom suburb of San Francisco. Pamphlets distributed by the Board of Trade in the 1880s and 1890s advertised Oakland as "largely a city of homes" where "almost every dwelling is provided with an ever-green lawn and an ever-blooming garden."[1] Oaklanders soon came to see the creation of parks and boulevards as a way to protect and enhance the appearance of their city, and thus the values of their own private property, and it was with an effort to improve upon and add to the city's parks that planning began in Oakland.

Oaklanders were not alone in that approach. Parks were often included in the agendas of proponents of city improvements and city plans during the late nineteenth and early twentieth centuries. Parks and boulevards were components in the Burnham Plan for San Francisco. They would become, as well, significant parts of the planning campaigns in Portland and Seattle. Taking their cue from landscape architects like Frederick Law Olmsted, planners throughout the nation saw parks as improving the urban landscape in myriad ways. As Oaklanders asserted, parks could enhance the value of nearby private property, thus boosting the city's tax base. Parks could also improve a city's economic base by attracting tourists and settlers. Social considerations were also important. As Burnham argued, parks could instill certain values and ways of thinking in those who used them, especially children. Parks could, as well, serve as alternatives to saloons and street gangs—an argument put forward especially in Seattle. A humanitarian concern could thereby mix with an economic one, the desire to combat disorderly conduct and crime.

As early as the 1860s, less than twenty years after the founding of Oakland, Olmsted, who was already well known nationally for his design of Central Park in New York and for his work on the capitol grounds of Washington, D.C., visited Oakland and recommended the establishment of a park system. Olmsted was in California to view Yosemite, which he was trying to convince Congress to preserve as a national park. While there, he agreed to

64

Oaklanders wanted a city of tree-lined streets and single-family houses. From the Robinson Plan for Oakland.

come to Oakland to design the Mountain View Cemetery; and he took advantage of his trip to call upon Oaklanders to establish a park system. Olmsted envisioned a belt of parks along the crest of the Oakland hills, extending down through the town along canyons and creeks. Nothing came of Olmsted's ideas at the time, but they would influence twentieth-century planners.[2]

Lake Merritt, a saltwater estuary connected to San Francisco Bay and extending inland into the center of Oakland, lay at the heart of subsequent plans to improve the city's parks. Private actions both aided and hampered the development of Lake Merritt as a recreation area. A private citizen, Dr. Samuel Merritt, formed the "lake" by damming its outlet to the bay in 1868. By the 1880s and 1890s, however, population growth in Oakland and the spread of private residences around the banks of Lake Merritt threatened the body of water with sewage.[3] For several years, Lake Merritt had, as one contemporary writer put it, "a reputation of being unhealthy on account of defective sewerage, which caused a great deal of sickness in the shape of diphtheria and low malarial fever."[4]

The city acquired Lake Merritt from its private owners in 1891, setting the stage for its possible development as a park. The first major effort to use public funds for park improvements in Oakland occurred in 1892. In that year the city council placed two park bond issues, each for $400,000, before the voters. One provided for the dredging of Lake Merritt and its encirclement by a scenic boulevard, according to plans drawn up by the city engineer. The other called for the draining of marshes in West Oakland and the conversion of the wetlands into a park, including areas for tennis, baseball, and football. Particularly noteworthy at a time when the playground movement was just beginning in the United States was the proposition that a part of the West Oakland park consist of "a large open meadow dotted here and there with groups of trees, and dedicated to the children for a play and picnic ground."[5]

The park bond issues won strong backing from Oakland's business organizations. The Board of Trade, the Federated Trades Association, and the Retail Clerks Association (an organization of middle-level store managers) came out for them. Employing arguments that would become the standard ones used by park advocates in Pacific Coast cities, members of those associations equated parks with economic gain. The president of the Board of Trade noted that the cost of the bonds was "not burdensome" when compared to the anticipated benefits. Similarly, one of Oakland's leading merchants, Hugo Abrahamson, claimed that "the building of a boulevard about Lake Merritt and the transformation of the West Oakland marsh into a park will attract people, and everything that draws people to the city makes business of all sorts better." Labor leaders also supported the bonds. The head of the Carpenters' Union explained that the passage of the bonds would "mean work and wages for a long period to several hundred men in all ranks of labor."[6]

Oakland's leading businessmen formed the Oakland Improvement League to push for the bonds. Its members equated business development with civic progress and quickly came to view approval of the park bonds as one way to place Oakland on an equal footing with its counterparts on the Pacific Coast and across the nation. Passage of the bonds would, they thought, signal that their city had arrived as a major force in America's growing urban network. Civic pride, as well as economic growth, was at stake. The organization's chairman summed up the reasons many businessmen thought the bonds should be approved in a pamphlet titled *Vote for Progress* published on the eve of the election:

> It will increase the volume of local trade, give work to our idle laboring men, stimulate private enterprise, and add a large sum of money in local circulation. Better than all, voting the bonds will give notice to the outside world that Oakland has taken up her march on the high road of progress. . . . We trust every citizen will sink all petty considerations and resolve to do his best to give Oakland her proper place among cities.[7]

Despite such support, the bonds failed to win approval. Like most of the bonds issued by Pacific Coast cities, they were general obligation bonds requiring a favorable two-thirds vote. Although a majority of voters favored the bonds, they did not secure the necessary two-thirds vote. Some voters feared that the city government might waste the money, while others were opposed to any possible increase in their tax rates. In spite of the defeat, the city government made some improvements to Lake Merritt over the next few years by constructing sewers and directing their outflow away from the lake into San Francisco Bay.

After being sidetracked by the depression of the mid-1890s, the issue of park improvements was revived in 1898 when the city council placed a park bond issue of $320,000, most of which was designated for the purchase and improvement of sixty-two acres on the shores of Lake Merritt, on the ballot. The city council, Board of Trade, and Merchants' Exchange all came out publicly for the bonds. As they had six years before, park bond proponents formed an umbrella committee—headed by the secretary of the Oakland Gas and Light Company and composed of merchants, manufacturers, city officials, lawyers, and the president of the Pacific Theological Seminary—to campaign for the bonds.

In public presentations and widely distributed broadsides, the committee members praised parks for their social and moral influences. "A park has a distinct influence in favor of public morality," claimed one advocate, for "in a public place, under the eyes of his fellows, surrounded by healthful outdoor influences, a person can not be engaged in anything very wrong." Moreover, he continued, "A park is a humanizing institution, because it brings all the people together. It is a neutral ground of ranks and classes. The poorest man owns as much of the public park as the richest. . . . But for it the two extremes in the social scale in our largest cities would never see each other."[8]

The expected economic benefits of parks also continued to win the attention of the supporters of the park bonds. Parks would increase the value of nearby private properties and, more generally, of land throughout Oakland. "Investment in parks has proven remunerative to every city which has been wise enough to make provision in this direction," explained one of the broadsides. "The purchase and improvement of this tract will add to the attractiveness of Oakland as a place of residence, and thus increase the value of every foot of land in the city." Still more was involved, for, as in 1892, bond supporters argued that nothing less than the fate of their city was at stake. They claimed that approval of the bonds would "show the world that we have faith in ourselves, faith in the future of our beautiful city."[9]

Nonetheless, the bonds again went down to defeat at the polls. As they had six years before, the park bonds won a simple majority but not the required two-thirds of the votes. With that defeat, the Oakland *Enquirer* concluded that Oakland had "lost its last opportunity to create a park on the shores of the lake."[10] Such predictions proved wrong. Oakland was just entering a period of hectic civic improvements.

The Robinson Plan for Oakland

As Oakland moved out from beneath the shadow of San Francisco in the opening years of the twentieth century, its residents turned to civic improvements and city planning as ways of claiming what they viewed as their rightful place in the sun. The Oak-

68

land Board of Trade continued to trumpet the city as a place where "many of the residences are palatial and . . . surrounded by either lawn or flowers" and as "a city of homes, commerce, culture and churches." Increasingly, however, the board advertised Oakland as a port city and manufacturing center: "the natural waterfront center of a state three times the size of New York" and "the terminus of all transcontinental railroads."[11] Oakland was hurt less than San Francisco by the 1906 earthquake. As Oakland's mayor observed, "The earthquake this morning visited upon our City a great calamity, yet it is a source of much satisfaction that we were spared from a conflagration and serious loss of life."[12] Oakland's rapid ascent as a center of trade and industry after the earthquake and fire of 1906 brought new concerns to the fore. More than in the past, Oaklanders concentrated on building the infrastructure needed for the continued development of their city.

Frank Mott led the city in its growth. What James Phelan was for San Francisco, Mott was for Oakland: a business leader who saw in politics a way to shape his city's future. A self-made man in the hardware business, Mott entered politics as a city councilman in 1894. Endorsed by both the Republicans and Democrats, he won election as mayor in 1905, a post he held until he stepped down ten years later. Like Phelan, Mott saw business and civic developments as naturally proceeding hand in hand. At the same time that he was mayor, Mott became deeply involved in real estate development, serving as the president of the Oakland Real Estate Board and the California State Realty Federation. If Mott was similar to Phelan in his outlook on civic development, his impact was greater. With fewer ethnic and socioeconomic divisions separating groups within his city, Mott proved more effective in making his desires reality.[13]

Enjoying immense popularity throughout Oakland, Mott acted as a progressive mayor. One urban historian has called Mott's administration "the very model of progressive city government."[14] Mott initiated civil service jobs in the city government and secured adoption of a new city charter. Concerned about city services, he reorganized the police and fire departments, built new water and sewer lines, placed electric wires underground, and installed new street lighting. Deeply interested in parks and civic improvements, Mott provided active governmental leadership in those areas. In 1905 and 1906, Mott, who been been a leader in the

69

1898 bond campaign, altered the city's method of administering its parks and initiated some improvements, including the dredging of Lake Merritt and the construction of Harrison Boulevard.[15] As was so often the case among Pacific Coast business and political leaders, civic pride, a desire to see his city accepted as a member of the nation's network of cities, motivated Mott. As a result of his actions, Mott could tell his fellow Oaklanders with considerable justification in his farewell speech in 1915, "We have come up out of a minor place to a position of strength, influence, well-being, comfort, and convenience among our sister cities."[16]

In one of his more far-reaching moves, Mott, with the concurrence of the city council, invited Charles Mumford Robinson to come to Oakland and draw up a plan for the city's future development. Robinson was a nationally known proponent of the city beautiful. In the late 1890s, Robinson had written a series of articles about municipal improvements for the *Atlantic Monthly,* and in 1899 he toured European cities to prepare a similar series for *Harper's Magazine.* From those experiences came Robinson's first book, *The Improvement of Cities and Towns,* in 1901, followed by a second volume, *Modern Civic Art,* just a few years later. In those widely read works Robinson popularized the idea that people could control and improve the physical environments of their cities. He espoused the notion that civic art joined utility to beauty, that there was "nothing effeminate [by which Robinson meant weak] and sentimental" about art and civic improvements—an argument that won praise from improvement groups and business organizations across the nation.[17]

One of the national leaders in the city beautiful movement, Robinson would eventually prepare some twenty-five city planning reports and in 1913 would be awarded the Chair of Civic Design at the University of Illinois. According to William Wilson, the leading historian of the city beautiful movement, Robinson "adopted a comprehensive view of the city" in all of his work. That is, Robinson "exempted no urban area from beautification effort."[18] Nonetheless, Robinson's vision, while broad for his time, was far from truly comprehensive, for many urban concerns simply lay beyond his ken.

After visiting Oakland several times in 1905 and 1906, Robinson drafted a plan for the city and submitted it to Mott in May 1906. Like the plans prepared for other Pacific Coast cities, the Robinson Plan for Oakland sought to cope with the consequences of urban growth. "Oakland can hardly fail now to increase even more rapidly than heretofore in population and in business," Robinson predicted in the preface to his plan. "You have to plan for a great city." Robinson further claimed that his plan was comprehensive. "Nor shall we be dealing with only esthetic needs," he declared. "Modern city building is a science as much as art [and] has to do also with social, moral, and industrial problems." As in his plans for other cities, Robinson asserted in his plan for Oakland that "beauty is not an ornament to be stuck on. Its essence lies in its structural utility."[19] Robinson certainly saw his plan as addressing the social and economic, as well as the aesthetic, needs of Oaklanders; for him all three types of concerns were closely intermixed.

In fact, Robinson's plan dealt mainly with the need for parks and boulevards. Much of the plan discussed the creation of large parks connected by drives and parkways. Robinson stressed the urgent need to make a park out of the land surrounding Lake Merritt and to build a boulevard around the lake. Robinson also called for the development of a three-hundred-acre park in Indian Gulch just to the northeast of the lake as a site for "picturesque and romantic walks and drives." From Indian Gulch a parkway would extend to Dimond Canyon and then on to East Oakland. Robinson urged that Oaklanders connect the proposed city park system with a still larger county park system. Beyond his suggestions for large parks, Robinson called for numerous smaller neighborhood parks and playgrounds as ornamental pieces to beautify their parts of the city and as recreation centers. Finally, Robinson urged the appointment of a park commission to oversee all of the developments.[20]

Robinson viewed the parks as helping Oakland both economically and socially. Noting that "Los Angeles, Portland, and Seattle have already had the courage to do and plan much more," he suggested that the new parks would aid Oakland in its rivalry with other Pacific Coast cities. The parks would also benefit property owners by serving as firebreaks and by leading to an increase in property values. Most important to Robinson, however, was the social impact of the parks. The parks would, he thought, "alleviate the hard conditions of crowded humanity" and bring together "all the people, high and low, rich and poor, without distinction."[21]

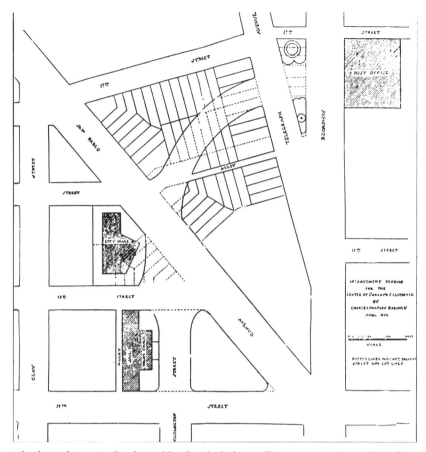

Charles Robinson's plan for Oakland included a small civic center. From the Robinson Plan for Oakland.

Although most of Robinson's plan dealt with park and boulevard proposals, it gave consideration to other matters. Robinson suggested the construction of a small civic center consisting of a city hall, post office, and police building at the intersection of San Pablo Avenue and Fourteenth Street. He also called for regulating billboards, removing wires over streets, improving street lighting, and replacing wooden street curbs with stone or concrete.[22]

Robinson's plan contained nothing revolutionary. Many of his ideas for parks had been foreshadowed by Olmsted's concepts

72

forty years earlier. Oaklanders had been talking about the need for a civic center for some time by 1906, and the other improvements suggested by Robinson had also long been under discussion. Only twenty pages long, the Robinson Plan for Oakland stood in sharp contrast to the ambitious remaking of San Francisco espoused by Daniel Burnham. It contained no wholesale street changes or plans for a grandiose civic center. Even more than the Burnham Plan, Robinson's plan ignored the housing needs of urban residents and did not intend to alter living arrangements in Oakland.

The relatively limited nature of the "Robinson Plan for Oakland" boded well for its adoption. So did the strong and effective political support given by Mayor Mott—again in marked contrast to the situation in San Francisco, where political divisions hindered the adoption of the Burnham Plan. Accepting the plan just a month after the San Francisco earthquake, Mott passed the plan on to the city council with the observation that it "is very comprehensive and contains many valuable and important suggestions. I commend it to your careful consideration."[23]

Civic Improvements in Oakland

Mott had the city council print and distribute numerous copies of Robinson's plan. Then, to gain firsthand knowledge of what other cities were doing in the realms of parks and planning, Mott spent several weeks touring New York, Boston, Kansas City, Cleveland, and Chicago. He returned to Oakland more convinced than ever that civic improvements were needed for his city.[24] Nor was he alone. The Oakland *Tribune* mounted a campaign to clean up the city in late 1906 and early 1907, observing that the condition of many of even the city's major streets was "a disgrace to the people of Oakland."[25] A letter to the editor of the newspaper captured the growing desire on the part of Oaklanders for a more beautiful city. "Can not a movement be started in Oakland to give houses generally a coat of paint and to clean up and repair sidewalks and fences," the writer asked "How much cheer would come to visitors if the houses were painted with bright shining colors?"[26]

The first major accomplishments based on Robinson's ideas materialized when voters approved a $992,000 bond issue for park improvements in 1907. Pushed by Mott, the city council, and virtually all of Oakland's leading businessmen, the bonds provided for the acquisition of ten pieces of property for park purposes, five of which bordered upon Lake Merritt.[27] Like Robinson, Oaklanders saw the development of parks as benefiting their city in a variety of ways, but they stressed the economic advantages and the fact that Oakland needed more and better parks to compete with other Pacific Coast cities for immigrants. An editorial in the Oakland *Tribune* summed up many of the reasons Oaklanders had come to think favorably of parks:

One of the positive signs that Oakland is preparing to take her position among the great cities of the Pacific Coast is the attention being paid to its external environment. . . . To induce growth and expansion people must be brought from the outside. To bring people from outside there must be attractions. . . . That which affords the most beauty and convenience will be the first to attract notice. . . . Oakland can do what Southern California has accomplished if it will.[28]

The bonds won a five-to-one majority. Oakland had developed considerably since bond issues had failed in the 1890s, and the passage of the park bonds in 1907 was seen as a matter of civic pride. The Oakland *Tribune* crowed that "the citizens of Oakland have demonstrated in a signal and practical manner that the spirit of progress dominates the community" and predicted that the bonds would "give Oakland a more beautiful and majestic appearance" that would "stimulate private improvement on a large scale."[29] Similarly, Mott noted with approval shortly after the election that "every municipality with any pretention at all in these days is giving much thought and money" to civic improvements. Parks, he thought, were "essential" to help "install us in the front rank of American municipalities."[30] The Chamber of Commerce asserted that "the Public Park System of Oakland, as at present outlined, is destined to make the city famous."[31] In an open letter to Oaklanders, Robinson also applauded the passage of the park bonds. "Apart from the aesthetic gain to the city," he claimed, parks "will so improve the value of adjacent and neighboring prop-erty that in the consequent rise in assessment values, they will quickly pay for themselves."[32]

Oakland continued to develop its parks over the next few years, though the city never went as far as Robinson had desired. In 1908 Oaklanders approved an additional $125,000 in park bonds, mainly to improve Lake Merritt.[33] A year later they voted to amend their city charter to create the park commission that Robinson had proposed.[34] A separate commission had been set up the previous year to develop playgrounds to help boys and girls grow into "strong healthy manhood or womanhood" by providing places where they could "meet with other children and indulge in the teamwork and tribal spirit that results from the playing of games."[35] By 1915 Oak-land possessed thirteen municipal playgrounds and twenty-seven schoolyard playgrounds where "athletics, games, plays, dancing . . . pageants and festivals" took place.[36]

From these beginnings with parks, Mott and his supporters moved on to other civic improvements. In his second inaugural address in 1907 Mott called upon Oaklanders to unite in a spirit of "municipal pride, patriotism and loyalty" to continue improving their city.[37] Mott had the strong support of business organizations, most notably the Chamber of Commerce and the Santa Fe Im-provement Association, a group of business leaders organized in 1907 to press for municipal improvements.[38]

Most importantly, Mott called for the construction of a new city hall. Civic pride continued to motivate him and his business sup-porters. Calling Oakland's present structure "unsafe" and "totally inadequate," Mott thought that "with the present growth and standing of our city it is in addition a serious reflection on us."[39] At Mott's urging, Oakland residents approved $1.15 million in bonds for a new city hall in 1909. Designed by a New York archi-tectural firm, the structure was to thrust upward eighteen stories as a skyscraper near the site for a civic center suggested in Robin-son's plan. Revolutionary in design for its time, the city hall was, Mott noted with approval, "out of the ordinary and conventional style" and would "attract notice everywhere and will put Oakland in the front ranks of modern cities."[40] President William Howard Taft laid the cornerstone in 1911 after a delay that had been prompted by the Oakland *Tribune* to protest the employment of eastern ar-chitects. City hall was completed three years later.[41]

The Oakland Civic Auditorium helped prepare the city for the Panama–Pacific International Exhibition. From the Hegemann Plan for Oakland and Berkeley.

Following their approval of the city hall bonds, Oaklanders voted favorably in 1911 on a $500,000 bond issue to fund the construction of a civic auditorium. Business groups campaigned vigorously for the bonds as being necessary for their city's economic advance. The auditorium was expected to help bring conventions, (many were expected to meet in conjunction with visits to San Francisco's Panama–Pacific International Exposition), capital, and businesses to Oakland. More generally, its backers claimed that the auditorium was needed to keep Oakland abreast of its urban rivals and to win acceptance for their city as a leading American metropolis. "If Oakland is to take its place in the ranks of progressive and up-to-date cities it must positively have such a building," the president of the Santa Fe Improvement Association asserted. "If it is desired to attract capital here and increase the population, then must Oakland have an auditorium."[42] The secretary of the Chamber of Commerce came out for the bonds for much the same reasons. The auditorium would be "a good investment" by attracting people to Oakland.[43] Oakland's residents approved the bonds, only to discover over the next three years that cost overruns made it impossible to construct the type of auditorium they desired for $500,000.[44]

As a consequence, the city council returned to the voters in 1914 to request an additional $500,000 to complete the structure.

Once again business groups led the campaign. The Chamber of Commerce organized a Progress and Prosperity Committee as its "militant arm" to work for the bonds; and the committee divided the city into wards, with a business leader in charge of the campaign for the bonds in each ward. Working with Mayor Mott and the councilmen, the businessmen launched a massive educational movement on behalf of the bonds.[45] As in 1911, those favoring the bonds appealed to the civic pride of Oaklanders. "The world is coming this way next year [a reference to the Panama-Pacific International Exposition] and Oakland cannot afford to have a steel structure proclaiming that the city is too poor to put a cover on its ribs," observed one. To leave the auditorium unfinished would, another noted, be "humiliating and discrediting to its citizenship."[46] The economic arguments—that the passage of the auditorium bonds would "make more work and more wages and better business"—were rolled out once again.[47] The bonds won approval by the scant majority of 139 votes out of 23,577 cast (unlike the park bonds and most other bonds, they required only a simple majority). Mayor Mott found the election result "most gratifying." After learning that the bonds had passed, members of the Chamber of Commerce and the Commercial Club "organized a parade, and headed by bands of music, marched through the business streets of the city."[48]

With more limited aims and benefiting from the strong backing of their mayor and city council, planning proponents more fully accomplished their goals in Oakland than did their counterparts in San Francisco. They made considerable progress: a new park system was laid out, a new city hall and a new auditorium were built, and smaller civic improvements were made. Nonetheless, Oaklanders were no more successful than San Franciscans in adopting a truly comprehensive plan for their city, as can be seen in their failure to follow a plan drafted by Werner Hegemann for the development of Berkeley and Oakland.

Hegemann came to the United States in 1912 at the request of the People's Institute of New York "to cooperate with American cities in the promotion of planning projects." Hegemann was already well known as the secretary of the Committee for the Architectural Development of Greater Berlin and as the general secretary of city planning exhibits in Berlin and Düsseldorf. As he traveled through cities of the East Coast and Midwest giving lectures and preparing planning reports, his reputation grew. Soon after his arrival in the East Bay in October 1913, he was invited by the city councils of Oakland and Berkeley to "inspect and report on conditions" in those cities. Published in 1915 under the joint auspices of governmental bodies—the city governments of Oakland and Berkeley, the Civic Art Commission of Berkeley, and the Board of Supervisors of Alameda County—and private business and civic organizations—the Oakland Chamber of Commerce, the Oakland Commercial Club, and the City Club of Berkeley— the Hegemann Plan was quite different from the Robinson Plan for Oakland.[49]

Hegemann was less interested in aesthetics and more concerned than Robinson with the economic and social conditions in the cities he studied and planned for. "If civic art is the sublime flower that can finally be hoped for," Hegemann explained, "the necessary roots, stems and leaves must be found in the economic, social, hygenic and recreation life of the communities."[50] Accordingly, most of his plan for Oakland and Berkeley consisted of detailed suggestions for the coordinated development of harbor improvements, changes in railroad routes, and the construction of commercial streets. All of the changes were needed, Hegemann asserted, to allow the East Bay to compete successfully as a center of trade and industry with San Francisco. Beyond those matters, Hegemann called for the creation of complete civic centers in Oakland and Berkeley and the development of a regional park system along the lines put forward by Robinson. Finally, Hegemann urged the building of better housing for the working classes, noting that "the settlement of the problems of housing for the masses of the population in the long run determines the fate of a city, its health, beauty, civic spirit, political texture."[51]

While portions of the Hegemann Plan were implemented over the years, the plan never won adoption as a unified, comprehensive guide for the development of the East Bay. In part, that failure was due to World War I, which disrupted planning efforts. It resulted as well from alterations occurring in the city planning movement itself. In 1915 the California legislature passed a City Planning Enabling Act that permitted municipalities to establish city planning commissions. The commissions could advise city governments on changes needed for the development of the cities. The legislation also allowed city councils to zone areas for

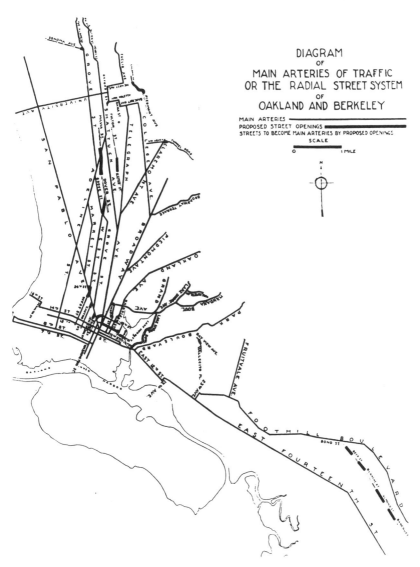

Major improvements in traffic flow were part of the Hegemann Plan for Oakland and Berkeley.

residential, commercial, and industrial use. (Los Angeles already possessed zoning ordinances, and a decision of the California Supreme Court upheld their validity in 1913.) Further legislation two years later strengthened the zoning powers of municipalities.[52]

Zoning became the vogue across America by the time of World War I. As the urban historian Mellior Scott has observed, at that time "popular interest began to focus on one phase of city planning—zoning to protect single-family residential areas from invasion by factories, stores, and apartment houses."[53] Zoning differed from the type of planning put forward by Burnham and Robinson. Zoning did not necessarily envision organically unified cities integrated around civic centers, functionally laid-out streets and harbors, and parks and boulevards. In the cities of some states, zoning could proceed before the preparation of any overall city plans. In Wisconsin and Minnesota, for example, zoning districts were established in cities simply upon the petitions of property owners.[54] Many in the nation's city planning movement deplored the spread of zoning for distracting attention from what they viewed as the real social and economic problems their cities faced. As Frank Backus, a New Yorker who specialized in the legal aspects of city planning, explained in 1914, "So far what we have done along districting lines has been, practically, housing without city planning instead of housing as an element of city planning, so little has districting been a part of the planning of the city as a whole, so little has it been used to aid in the solution of more general city problems."[55]

In California citywide land use plans—plans setting aside areas for residential, commercial, and industrial use—generally had to accompany the establishment of zoning districts within cities. Nonetheless, the spread of zoning led to a major shift in emphasis in city planning away from comprehensive plans encompassing civic centers, new streets and harbors, and parks and boulevards. It was not that zoning destroyed what had already had been accomplished along those lines, as it was that the growing interest in zoning precluded further elaboration after the war. Zoning proposals tended to be initiated by real estate men interested primarily in protecting their private investments and developments; they were often supported, however, by home owners eager to protect their property values. The embrace of zoning represented something of a turning away from planning as a weapon in the

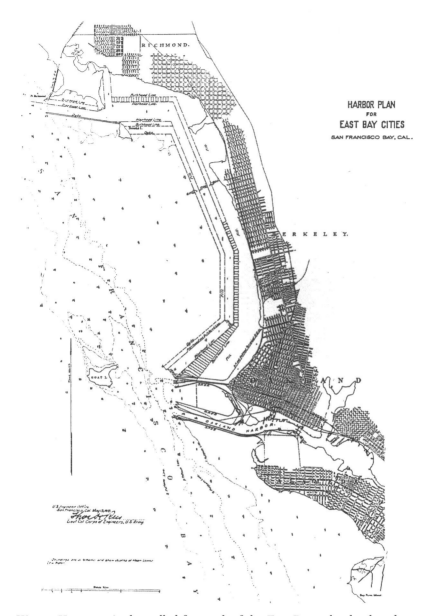

Werner Hegemann's plan called for much of the East Bay to be developed as a unified geographic region. From the Hegemann Plan for Oakland and Berkeley.

81

fight for urban dominance on the Pacific Coast toward the use of city planning as a tool to solve specific, limited urban problems.

Taking their lead from the residents of Los Angeles, Oaklanders adopted a zoning ordinance in 1914. Introduced to the city council by Mayor Mott, the ordinance set up an industrial zone within which manufacturing concerns would be located. As explained by Mott, the ordinance was "aimed at the inclusion of all industries within definite areas for the protection of people who desire their homes to be located far from the annoyances of shops and factories."[56]

City Planning Begins in Los Angeles

In Los Angeles, as in Oakland, one of the original goals of city improvements and planning was the protection of suburban districts for private homes. As we have seen, Los Angeles developed in part as a result of health and real estate booms. Like Oakland, and in contrast to San Francisco, Los Angeles was a residential city of private homes: and the preservation and furtherance of the "rurban" characteristic of the city was one of the aims of many planners. In 1915 a widely distributed pamphlet put out by the Chamber of Commerce observed that "here may be found beautiful rural homes, whose owners are within touch of social life, and enjoy the best features of the city and country combined."[57] As Los Angeles entered the twentieth century, however, the commercial and industrial bases that it developed also called for attention. The congestion of the downtown area in particular attracted notice and generated attempts to relieve it.

Parks, which had figured so prominently in the planning movement in Oakland, were of lesser significance in Los Angeles. Some wealthy citizens donated lands to the city for park purposes. The three thousand acres given by Griffith J. Griffith in 1891 became the basis for the city's outstanding Griffith Park. Perhaps because the city expanded outward rapidly via real estate subdivisions, however, no park movement as intense as Oakland's materialized. Rather, most residents hoped to find a bit of nature in their own backyards.

Nonetheless, in 1911 a plan to construct a major parkway won

Like Oakland, Los Angeles was a city of bungalows. From the Robinson Plan for Los Angeles.

consideration. It would extend along the Arroyo Seco River from the Angeles National Forest through Pasadena to Los Angeles, where it would join a metropolitan parkway system. In his report on the proposed system, Laurie Cox, the landscape engineer who designed it, argued that the parkway would add to "the health and happiness of the citizens and to the prosperity of the municipality itself." Moreover, it would help place Los Angeles on par with "Boston, Chicago, Kansas City, Washington, Minneapolis, Philadelphia" and other metropolises as a leading American city.[58] Cox presented his report to the Los Angeles Park Commission at a mass meeting presided over by the City Club, a nonpartisan organization pushing for progressive politics. Those at the meeting resolved that the City Club appoint a committee to work with city officials for park improvements, and over the next few years a number of improvements were made. As early as the summer of 1912, the San Francisco *Examiner* could report with envy that Los Angeles "has been going forward, and at an amazing pace" in the construction of parks. San Franciscans could, the newspaper concluded, "gain a lesson in civic progress" from this "'noble' park plan."[59]

In the end, Los Angeles's park and parkway plans were only incompletely implemented. Most disappointing to many park proponents was the failure to turn Wilshire Boulevard within Los Angeles into a parkway. It became, instead, a commercial highway strip. By 1930 the park system of Los Angeles consisted of fifty-three hundred acres and compared favorably in size to those of other Pacific Coast cities. However, as the leading historian of Los Angeles, Robert Fogelson, has concluded, it "fell far short of the planners' aspirations."[60]

Rather than originate in a park and boulevard movement, the planning campaign in Los Angeles found its origins in other sources. One was the attempt by leading businessmen and professionals, banded together as the Municipal Art Commission, to work for the beautification of Los Angeles. Another lay in zoning. Los Angeles was one of the first cities in America to adopt citywide zoning codes.

The Robinson Plan for Los Angeles

Beautification and improvement efforts began in 1903 with the establishment of the Municipal Art Commission. Including within its membership the nationally respected architect John Parkinson, the commission both tried to bring about alterations on its own and sought to advise the city government on the need for changes. The commission tried to secure better cleaning and lighting for public streets and sought to influence the design of public buildings. Members of the commission also tried through speeches and publications to popularize the cause of civic improvements.[61] In addition to their actions as members of the Municipal Art Commission, merchants, real estate developers, and bankers labored through their own business organizations to improve their city. From its founding in 1903, the Los Angeles Realty Board worked to clean up vacant lots, limit the height of buildings, and promote public art.[62] In 1905 a group of downtown businessmen sought to donate land valued at $200,000 to the city for a civic center, only to be rebuffed by the city government, which had not yet decided what shape a center should take or at what site it should be built.[63]

As it developed, the city planning campaign became associated with the more general progressive reform movement in Los Angeles. "City and regional planning," Fogelson has written, "emerged as an integral part of progressivism in Los Angeles after 1900."[64] That many of the same people, such as City Club president Meyer Lissner, were active in both progressive politics and city planning is not surprising. City planning shared certain goals with urban progressivism in Los Angeles: the creation of a populace unified by a sense of community, economic growth for the city, and better living conditions for its residents. As it unfolded during nearly two decades in Los Angeles, progressivism came to embrace devices designed to make city politics more efficient and honest by taking political control away from machine politicians. In addition, it endorsed some forms of municipal ownership of public utilities, and the passage of ordinances aimed at closing saloons, ending prostitution, and eliminating racetrack betting.[65]

The combined efforts of the Municipal Art Commission and the business groups popularized the cause of planning and improvements in Los Angeles. Dana Bartlett, a minister born in Maine who was serving as a clergyman and social worker in Los Angeles, caught well the desires of many involved in the civic improvement movement.[66] In a book he published in 1907 titled *The Better City*, he observed, "Ugliness has no commercial or ethical value." Rather, a beautiful city would be prosperous and would have a favorable moral impact upon its inhabitants. Bartlett called for the planting of trees to make Los Angeles "a forest city," the building of streets along the natural contours of the land rather than along the design of a gridiron, and the development of parks, including one along the Arroyo Seco River.[67]

In early 1906, the Municipal Art Commission recommended that Charles Robinson be retained by the city government to "lay out a plan for the beautifying of Los Angeles and the surrounding country." After some further discussion among themselves, members of the commission convinced the city council to hire Robinson in the spring of 1907. With the council's approval, the commission invited Robinson to visit Los Angeles and offer "such suggestions and recommendations for its improvement and beautification as were practicable in the limited time allotted." In the meantime, the commission solicited and received suggestions on improvements from the mayor, the park commission, the city forester, the Chamber of Commerce, the Real Estate Board, the Architects and Engineers Association, and the Merchants' and Manufacturers' Association. Robinson accepted the invitation and came to Los Angeles for three weeks in November 1907. After touring the city with members of the commission and considering the suggestions forwarded to him from other groups, Robinson presented his ideas to a meeting of the Municipal Art Commission in late 1907.[68]

Like his plan for Oakland, Robinson's plan for Los Angeles was limited in scope. While he gave consideration to street and transportation improvements, Robinson again dealt mainly with proposals for parks, boulevards, and a civic center. Robinson restricted his efforts in another way as well. He looked only at "those portions of the city in which conditions were most rapidly becoming fixed," that is, "the business district and all the more thickly settled parts of Los Angeles."[69] Although restricted in those ways, the Robinson Plan was not limited in any financial sense. "I set myself no goal in dollars to be expended," Robinson noted in the introduction to his plan. "I assumed that Los Angeles was big enough and rich enough, and brave enough and had enough confidence in itself, to do what was necessary and worthwhile." Robinson did not, however, expect all of his proposals to be implemented at once. "Some of them will stretch over a term of many years," he thought.[70]

In looking at the downtown, Robinson found an area that had grown up "in a swift and unsystematic" way, a district that was "jammed and crowded into narrow streets . . . unrelieved by open spaces." He proposed to remedy the situation partially through the construction of a union railroad station where the Alameda station then stood on Central Avenue. The new station would, Robinson thought, both "impress strangers" through a "dignified and splendid" entrance and relieve traffic congestion in the downtown area.[71] To further dignify and open up the downtown, Robinson urged the construction of a civic center, consisting of a post office, county courthouse, city hall, and several smaller structures, at the intersection of Temple, Spring, and Main streets. Open spaces and gardens would separate the buildings. Robinson noted that a private bank was already going up on one of the sites in the area for which he proposed the center but concluded that "it has at least the merit of rising like a warning finger . . . as if to

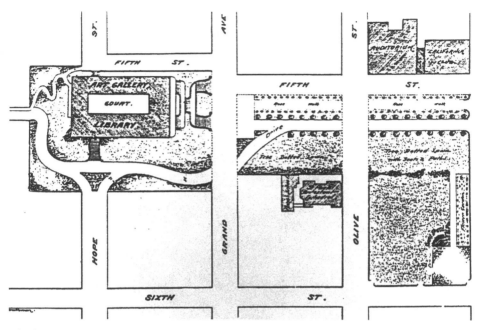

Charles Robinson's plan anticipated a new public library and civic center. From the Robinson Plan for Los Angeles.

caution the citizens of Los Angeles that if they desire to gain big effects and do big things in the building of their city it is not safe to delay the acquirement of the necessary land."[72] Robinson believed that the civic center would function in part "to dignify and emphasize the historic old Plaza" inherited from Spanish times, which was located just a few blocks away. He lamented that the "quaint little Plaza" was neglected and urged its connection to a large hillside park that he proposed developing nearby.[73]

From his consideration of the downtown, Robinson proceeded to recommend a park and boulevard system. He called for a large Central Park between Fifth and Sixth streets. Here would be located an art gallery and public library on a hill, with buildings whose "white columns showing from below against the blue California sky" would have a "Grecian" effect.[74] Boulevards would spread out to connect parks as "links in the chain" throughout Los Angeles. The boulevards would serve two purposes. They would

87

be places of rest and repose as "pleasure drives," and they would be "utilitarian to the extent that they are to furnish convenient and easy access between the various residential sections and between these and the business section."[75] Figueroa Street, Sunset Boulevard, Occidental Boulevard, Los Feliz Road, Wilshire Boulevard, and a drive along Arroyo Seco all attracted Robinson's attention as possible parkways.

Robinson also dealt with smaller, less encompassing matters. He proposed better street lighting for the downtown district, the beautification of street intersections and the entrances to tunnels, and the abolition of fences separating private residential lots as a way of making "one park of many . . . for the good of all." The planting of trees, and improvements to playgounds and schoolyards "because of the effect on children and through them on homes," also won Robinson's support.[76] Robinson especially decried the imposition of "Chicago-like gridiron street systems" on the varied topography of Los Angeles through "the mistaken greed and ignorance of real estate speculators." Robinson thought that such developers failed to understand that "beautiful winding roads that follow the contour" could both beautify Los Angeles and increase the value of their private real estate holdings, and he called upon city officials "to check the tendency."[77]

Robinson closed his report by urging the residents of Los Angeles make their city the "'Paris of America,'" a city with a "gay outdoor life." It was necessary, Robinson wrote in conclusion, "not to be simply big; but to be beautiful as well."[78] As did his plan for Oakland, Robinson's plan for Los Angeles differed considerably from the Burnham Plan for San Francisco. While both Burnham and Robinson were interested in beautification, Burnham was more the engineer. The detailed street designs of the Burnham Plan were for the most part absent in the Robinson Plan for Los Angeles. Nor was there any real attempt to understand the functional relationships between the different elements of a city that lay at the heart of the Burnham Plan.

As in his designs for Oakland, Robinson was conservative in his planning for Los Angeles. Robinson claimed that he planned for "the city as a unit," but he envisioned few of the major urban changes called for by Burnham for San Francisco or by those who sought to remake Portland and Seattle.[79] Robinson appealed to the civic pride of the residents of Los Angeles in seeking the

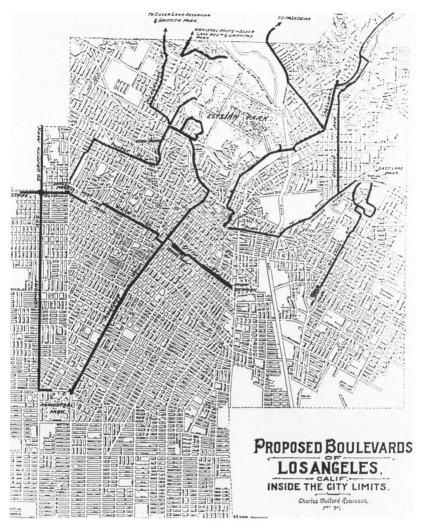

Charles Robinson's plan called for the construction of numerous boulevards. From the Robinson Plan for Los Angeles.

acceptance of his plans there. Only through planning could Los Angeles join cities across the nation as an equal. After noting that St. Paul, St. Louis, Denver, and other cities were preparing for the future through city planning, Robinson concluded that the "time for carrying out the plans rests with the business sense and civic pride of the citizens of Los Angeles."[80]

Progress on the implementation of Robinson's plan for Los Angeles was, however, painfully slow. Planning proponents lacked the political push of a Mayor Mott to bring the plan to fruition. Nor was there the sense of urgency that existed in San Francisco after its disaster. The Municipal Art Commission accepted Robinson's report on Los Angeles enthusiastically and voted immediately to forward the plan to the mayor and city council. There the plan lay. Not until 1909 did the city government appropriate funds to publish and distribute copies of the plan.[81] Only in August 1910 did the city council pass a resolution urging the mayor to appoint a committee to "consider the needs of the City" and to "develop a comprehensive plan whereby Los Angeles may develop her material improvement along artistic as well as practical lines."[82] The mayor set up a fifteen-member committee a short time later, but, strapped for funds and hurt by political infighting, it accomplished nothing.

In 1911 at the instigation of the harbor commissioner and at the invitation of the city council, Bion Arnold (the same engineer who prepared a transportation plan for San Francisco) drew up a plan for transportation improvements in the Los Angeles region. Meyer Lissner, a member of the Los Angeles Board of Public Utilities, and thus by city ordinance also a member of the Board of Harbor Commissioners, was instrumental in having the report prepared. Designed to allow Los Angeles "to reap the benefit from its harbor which it should receive when the Panama Canal is opened," the plan encompassed suggestions for a municipal railroad, local street railroads, interurban railroads, and mass transit facilities.[83] Arnold argued forcefully for the economic benefits of his plan. He claimed that "there is nothing that will advertise a city better, affect the value of real estate more widely and leave a more lasting impression on a community than a comprehensive City and District Plan." However, little came of his efforts.[84] Further abortive attempts to establish city planning commissions took place in 1913 and 1917, but not until 1920 was such a commission set up, then mainly to deal with zoning matters.[85]

The accomplishments of those desiring city planning along the lines of Robinson's ideas for Los Angeles were therefore limited. Parks were created, but only on a piecemeal basis. The city never acquired a park and boulevard system similar to that recommended by Robinson. For years controversies engulfed efforts to construct a civic center, as different groups argued about location, cost, and design. Typical was the failure of a bond issue in 1912 to build a new city hall on Temple Square, near where Robinson had recommended. Though favored by downtown real estate interests, the proposition generated opposition in the form of "conservative business sentiment" that thought that Los Angeles was already heavily bonded for other purposes. The city hall bonds failed to win approval.[86] When voters did finally approve a $7.5 million bond issue to build a civic center in 1922, they chose a compromise site deemed by the historian Fogelson as having serious "aesthetic shortcomings."[87]

Planners proved more successful in winning new supplies of water for their city, thereby allowing its continued expansion. While businessmen led attempts to implement Robinson's plan and were in the forefront of zoning efforts in Los Angeles, city officials spearheaded the drive to acquire water. As accurately portrayed in the movie *Chinatown*, ex-mayor Fred Eaton and city water engineer William Mulholland secretly purchased water rights for Los Angeles in the Owens River Valley during the early 1900s (a select group of businessmen, probably tipped off about those moves, purchased land at the southern end of the terminus for a projected aqueduct from the Owens River Valley to Los Angeles). Pushed by city officials and backed by most business interests, nearly $25 million in aqueduct bonds won approval from the city's voters. Completed in 1913, the aqueduct amply supplied the water needs of Los Angeles for years; and the city successfully implemented a policy of water-based expansion that increased its size from 43 to 442 square miles between 1906 and 1930. Project funding also greatly increased the debt of city residents, as "Los Angeles deliberately taxed and spent its way to growth."[88] By 1913 city property taxes, on a per capita basis, were the fourth highest in the United States. As funding strained their resources, the residents of Los Angeles demurred for a time from paying for what they viewed as less essential projects such as the civic center.

Los Angeles as a Pioneer in Zoning

Zoning represented another major approach to city improvement and planning. Real estate speculation played an important role in the development of Los Angeles. By 1930 Los Angeles was home to more than 6 percent of the nation's real estate agents, and one-seventh of the city's work force was directly involved in construction and real estate activities.[89] Real estate men were more important in city planning activities in Los Angeles than in any other Pacific Coast center. Relying first on voluntary measures, they soon turned to zoning ordinances to try to control the shape of their city's growth. In zoning they saw a precise form of planning that was more effective in protecting residential developments than was comprehensive planning, which involved civic centers, parks, and streets. They saw as well a means that they thought was less expensive.

Real estate developers had long used restrictive covenants to protect the value of lots in their subdivisions in Los Angeles, but it was in 1904 that they first succeeded in having the city council pass an ordinance creating a residential district in which some industrial activities were prohibited. While largely ineffective in practice, the ordinance suggested the possibilities of control inherent in land-use zoning.[90]

In 1908 the residents of Los Angeles replaced their zoning ordinance of four years before with two much more extensive ones. The ordinances are now accepted by many urban historians as the beginning of modern zoning in the United States, preceding the better known New York statute by eight years. While the first of the 1908 ordinances mapped out three large areas in Los Angeles in which most industrial operations would be forbidden, the second ordinance defined the areas in which industries would be allowed. Strongly pushed by the Los Angeles Realty Board as one way to revive temporarily slumping sales in real estate, the ordinances were intended to assure prospective lenders and home purchasers that Los Angeles would be a residential paradise of spacious homes in quiet, clean surroundings.[91]

Business opposition to the ordinances, especially that of Los Angeles's budding industrialists, limited their effectiveness. Seven major industrial districts, mainly along the Los Angeles River, were soon set up, with most of the rest of the city zoned for residential use. The zoning survived court tests to provide a model for the spread of zoning to Oakland and some other California cities.[92] Within Los Angeles, however, the results of zoning soon disappointed zoning advocates. The problem, from the viewpoint of those favoring the strict enforcement of zoning, was that the city council granted too many exemptions—more than one hundred by 1915, ranging in scope from a single city lot to a large section of the central business district.[93]

As the number of exemptions grew, some realtors initiated a movement to revise the zoning ordinances. A precipitating factor was the invasion in 1919 of the west side residential neighborhoods of Wilshire and West Lake by a clothing factory. At a meeting in 1920, a coalition of business groups formed to press for stricter zoning: members of the Chamber of Commerce, who were concerned that enough land be set aside for industrial purposes, the Realty Board, whose members wanted to protect residential areas, and members of other business groups. Together they called on the city council to set up a City Planning Commission to reconcile matters. The city council passed an enabling ordinance, and in 1921 the mayor appointed a fifty-one-member City Planning Commission composed of representatives from seventeen business and civic groups.[94] One of the first actions the commission took was to devise a new zoning plan based on five types of districts: single-family residential, multiple-family residential, commercial, light industrial, and heavy industrial.[95]

In taking that action, the City Planning Commission thrust Los Angeles back into its position as a "zoning pioneer," for Los Angeles became America's first large city to establish a separate category for single-family residences.[96] The goal the Realty Board had of preserving Los Angeles as a residential city was, nonetheless, only partly met. The growth of the city continued to outstrip efforts to control it. Only small parts of the city were actually zoned for single-family residential use. Moreover, zoning exemptions continued to be made. Throughout the 1920s, the City Planning Commission spent more than 80 percent of its time processing applications for zoning changes or exemptions, and most requests won approval. The only partial success of the Realty Board is not surprising. Its two hundred members in 1921 were only part of the real estate profession in Los Angeles. More speculative developers and builders opposed zoning restrictions. Then too other business groups did not fully embrace strict zoning. As they had in San Francisco, divisions among businessmen hindered the development of city planning—in this case in the form of zoning—in Los Angeles.[97]

The City Planning Commission did, however, prepare the way for future planning efforts in Los Angeles. In 1923 some of its members participated in the formation of the Los Angeles Regional Planning Commission, one of the first regional planning bodies established in the United States. Two years later, the City Planning Commission was itself changed into a smaller, adequately funded body with heightened political clout.[98] According to its director, the commission was designed to be "a coordinating medium through which all agencies . . . which contribute to the physical development of the community shall be focussed in a single attack upon the task of building a city of tomorrow."[99]

Brave words those. As in times past, however, population and spatial growth continued to outpace planning efforts. The rapid adoption of the automobile combined with a land boom in the 1920s to thwart attempts to control the city's decentralized expansion. Then too the residents of Los Angeles, for the most part, wanted that type of growth. The suburban bungalow with its own yard remained the ideal. Not surprisingly, a 1925 proposal to spend $133 million on public transit facilities, including twenty-six miles of subway lines and eighty-five miles of elevated tracks, got nowhere.[100] In 1949 an urban planner could still lament, "Is it unreasonable to expect that some planning agency representing the entire Los Angeles area should be preparing a master plan for the future development of the whole area?"[101]

The California Harbor Controversy

Even as they grappled with the issues of parks, streets, and civic centers, the business leaders of Oakland and Los Angeles worked through politics to improve their harbors. In these endeavors they were joined by their counterparts in San Francisco.

Efforts to improve harbors were often a part of the general planning work of the cities—as they were, as well, in Seattle and Portland. Although they were not included in Robinson's plans for Oakland and Los Angeles, many planning advocates saw better harbor facilities as a necessary component of comprehensive city planning. Planning proponents envisioned better harbor facilities connected to improved intracity street and transportation systems as a way of making more efficient the economic workings of their cities. Proponents, especially merchants and shippers, thought improved harbors would bring prosperity to them and their cities. They believed the improvements would also win national recognition for their cities and move them ahead of their urban rivals on the Pacific Coast.

Planning advocates viewed harbor improvements as especially important in light of the imminent completion of the Panama Canal. Only if their cities were well prepared, could they take advantage of the tremendous increase in trade and immigration they were sure would result from the opening of the canal. As the completion of the Panama Canal neared, rivalry intensified for the ocean trade passing through California; and that rivalry led to a spate of harbor improvements.

San Pedro, which landlocked Los Angeles annexed as its outlet to the ocean in 1908, possessed only an unprotected roadstead. In addition to the physical problem of constructing a harbor, there was the obstacle of the Southern Pacific Railroad. That corporation, which had brought prosperity to Los Angeles with one hand, threatened to throttle it by its control over the harbor at San Pedro with the other. In a twenty-year contest involving lengthy court battles and lobbying in the state and national legislatures, the Southern Pacific attempted to maintain its hold over Los Angeles's outlet to the sea. In 1911, however, the California State Supreme Court ruled in favor of the city and against the railroad that the tidelands were state property. Meanwhile, construction of an artificial harbor had been started by Los Angeles, and in 1910 an outer breakwater had been completed. The future of Los Angeles seemed assured, for all that remained to be done for the city to possess its own harbor was to transfer the title to the tidelands from the state to the city.[102]

Oakland faced an analogous situation. In 1910 court decisions and political actions led by Mayor Mott broke the control that

95

Southern Pacific had long held over that city's waterfront, and the city's residents readily approved bond issues for harbor improvements. In 1911 a leading San Francisco newspaper enviously called Oaklanders' actions "a bold stoke that seems to partake almost of egotism" and urged San Francisco merchants to emulate their fellows across the bay.[103] As in the case of Los Angeles, all that remained to be done was to pass ownership of the tidelands from the state to the city.[104]

San Francisco merchants viewed the development of rival harbors at Los Angeles and Oakland with alarm and, like other Pacific Coast businessmen, hoped to improve their harbor to prepare for the opening of the Panama Canal. As one advocate of harbor improvements lamented in 1911, San Francisco's facilities "are inadequate to handle the commerce of the port." He warned, "Unless San Francisco sees fit during the next four years to provide additional dockage facilities, the vast trade of the Panama Canal will have to go elsewhere."[105] As another explained, "All seaports are competitors with all other seaports on the same coast." Noting that "Los Angeles and Oakland have adopted the policy of taxation" to pay for harbor improvements, he urged San Franciscans to do the same.[106]

Making any changes to the San Francisco waterfront was complicated, however, because a State Board of Harbor Commissioners appointed by the governor controlled the port. Moreover, bond issues for the improvement of San Francisco's harbor had to win approval from the state legislature and then gain a majority in a statewide referendum. When San Francisco had been the only major port in California, this system had worked fairly well; but, as other ports rose to prominence, San Franciscans complained that state regulation hurt them. San Franciscans feared that they might lose control of the board and recognized as well that, as time went on, they would have less and less control over the passage of bond issues essential to their port's development.[107]

The contest for California's ocean traffic exploded in the 1911 state legislative session. When representatives from Los Angeles and Oakland introduced a bill tranferring the state-held tidelands to their cities, San Franciscans rallied as a unit in opposition, believing that, should the measure pass, Oakland and Los Angeles might set port charges lower than their own. The deadlock was resolved in a private meeting between representatives of the Los

Angeles Chamber of Commerce and the business organizations of San Francisco. San Franciscans agreed to withdraw their opposition in return for pledges of support on future bond issues for improvements to their harbor and for backing San Francisco as the site for a world's fair in 1915. Several days after the conference, members of San Francisco's merchant bodies wired their city's political representatives in Sacramento to vote for the tidelands measure, and it passed without dissent. Nonetheless, the compromise worried San Francisco merchants, and with good reason.[108]

Even as the political situation remained uncertain, merchants in Oakland and Los Angeles worked with city officials to improve their cities' harbors. In Los Angeles five bond elections between 1909 and 1932 raised $30 million to improve the city's harbor (the bonds won a needed two-thirds vote in each election). The funds financed the building of breakwaters, wharves, piers, docks, bridges and highways—all designed, as the Harbor Bond Campaign Committee of 1919 put it, to "make Los Angeles one of the great seats of world commerce."[109] Oaklanders, led by Mott, similarly approved bond issues to improve their harbor. Their activities proved successful. Within little more than a decade, Los Angeles handled the most freight tonnage of any Pacific Coast port and was third (after New York and Philadelphia) in terms of freight tonnage nationally.[110] Oakland was not far behind, rapidly overhauling San Francisco.

While the goal of comprehensive city planning encompassing parks, civic centers, new streets, and improved harbors was imperfectly realized in Oakland and Los Angeles, the results of their early planning efforts were, nonetheless, substantial. Oaklanders probably accomplished the most, in part because their goals were more modest than in Los Angeles, at least initially. Even more importantly, those supporting civic improvements and planning received strong, steadfast political support from their city's businessman mayor, Frank Mott. Then, too, Oakland's growth slowed a bit after 1910, giving residents a chance to catch up with and control their city's expansion—in marked contrast to the continuing very rapid growth in Los Angeles. Nonetheless, achievements in Los Angeles were meaningful, especially in realms of harbor construction and the acquisition of new water supplies—items that nearly all Los Angeles residents could agree were absolutely necessary for their city's future growth.

4

Seattle and the Bogue Plan

▼

In March 1912, members of Seattle's city council presented to the voters a city plan prepared by the engineer Virgil Bogue. Like Daniel Burnham in his planning for San Francisco, Bogue thought big in his efforts to remake Seattle. The Bogue Plan envisioned a metropolis of one million, a city with four times the population Seattle then possessed. The plan encompassed harbor improvements, major changes in the city's street and transportation systems, the building of a civic center in a new part of town, and the construction of an extensive park and boulevard system. Altogether the Bogue Plan embraced an area of 150 square miles. One of the more detailed city plans drawn up in the Progressive Era, the Bogue Plan was highly engineered, offering technical solutions to many of the problems of growth.

The experiences of Seattleites with the Bogue Plan reveal a great deal both about the origins, development, and demise of city planning movements in the Progressive Era. Seattle's planning drive, like those in San Francisco, Oakland, and Los Angeles, had varied origins. More than in the planning campaigns in California, however, professional architects and engineers led the initial phases of the planning movement in Seattle. Nonetheless, business groups were important from the first and grew greatly in importance as Seattle's planning campaign progressed. Although Seattle's business organizations could agree on a general need for city planning, they were deeply divided on its specifics. Those divisions, together with cleavages separating business bodies from other groups in Seattle, prevented the adoption of the Bogue Plan. While significant portions of the plan were put in place piecemeal, the plan as a whole failed to secure approval. The defeat of the Bogue Plan, like that of the Burnham Plan in San Francisco, illustrates well the limits of Progressive-Era planning in a pluralistic society.[1]

Parks and Expositions

As was the case in Oakland, the initial impetus for planning in Seattle revolved around creating a unified system of parks and boulevards.[2] Seattle acquired its first public parks during the 1880s, and in 1888 a three-man park board was set up by the city government to administer them. In 1892 E. O. Schwagerl—a professional engineer, architect, and landscape gardener—became Seattle's first superintendent of parks. Schwagerl had helped landscape the Paris Universal Exposition in 1867 and the Philadelphia Centennial Exposition in 1876, had drafted the plans for park and boulevard systems in Cleveland and St. Louis, and had worked on cemetery designs in a number of cities.[3]

Shortly after assuming his duties in Seattle, Schwagerl put forward a plan for the construction of a system of parks and boulevards throughout the city. Central to his plan was a "continuous boulevard, from 150 to 300 feet wide" encircling Seattle from north to south. From the "grand drive" smaller boulevards and parks would branch off at various points. Schwagerl argued for the quick adoption of his plan on economic grounds. He claimed that with the construction of the boulevard surrounding Seattle "a large area of now useless land would immediately become the property of capitalists, whose sagacity would at once lead them to

99

make improvements in conformity with the plan decided on by the municipal authorities, and a fresh and promising field would thus be be opened for enterprise and the profitable employment of labor."[4]

Schwagerl revealed his ideas at a meeting sponsored by the Seattle Chamber of Commerce in September 1892. Attended by "representative business men and leading citizens of Seattle," the gathering heard Schwagerl outline "his comprehensive plan for a system of parks and boulevards" and listened to Seattle's mayor speak "very forcibly in favor of it."[5] Over the next few years the city's park commissioners pressed for the adoption of Schwagerl's scheme. In doing so, they broadened their arguments to include a mixture of aesthetic, moral, and economic claims— foreshadowing many of the arguments used by Seattle's city planning proponents in the early twentieth century.

Matters of civic pride and economic development headed the commissioners' list of the reasons why Schwagerl's plan should be implemented. Parks were needed for Seattle to take its place as a major American city and as the leading city of the Pacific Northwest. The commissioners often spoke of "the necessity for the City of Seattle to avail itself of the prerogative found indispensable in other cities, of having its system of parks and boulevards." They frequently commented upon "the enormous importance of a proper system of parks" to Seattle whose "destiny" was to be "the metropolis of the North Pacific coast." Moreover, like Schwagerl, the commissioners believed that parks would spur Seattle's economic growth. Parks would boost real estate values by attracting "a swarm of people of all trades, professions and vocations" to Seattle. Even more importantly, parks would attract capital necessary for Seattle's economic growth, for, the commissioners bluntly stated, "park cities become centers towards which money tends."[6]

More was at stake than economic growth, for Seattle's aesthetic and social development was, the park commissioners believed, also involved. After noting that "the natural verdure around Lake Washington is still in its maiden beauty," they warned that unless actions were soon taken, areas suitable for parks and boulevards would be irretrievably lost to the woodsman's axe and urban expansion. Such an eventuality would be most unfortunate, the commissioners continued, for parks were much more than simply beautiful ornaments for a city. Like park proponents in Oakland, they saw parks as an uplifting moral force. They claimed, "There is probably no factor among civilized nations that ranks so high in the real education and refinement of the masses generally as public parks and grounds." Parks, they continued, "cleansed the mind, [and] so purified the life and rescued the family from the slums and the degradation to which they were formerly tending." Parks, in short, would be of "incalculable importance . . . in humanizing and refining the community."[7]

Despite the prevalence of such sentiments, little immediately came of Schwagerl's ideas. New parklands continued to be acquired, but no comprehensive park and boulevard system resulted. Seattleites were too preoccupied with more pressing concerns involved in building their city—regrading hills, laying water and sewer lines, and extending streets—to construct Schwagerl's unified scheme of parks. Schwagerl's plan simply appeared too far-reaching for Seattle's resources. As Schwagerl himself admitted in 1894, at a time when Seattle was wallowing in the trough of a nationwide business depression, "the general plans proposed during the past two years have proved to be so comprehensive and vast in extent as to render commencement along these lines too difficult for the present." Despite repeated pleas from Schwagerl and the park commissioners that "some system should be adopted at once," little of significance was accomplished until the twentieth century.[8]

Finally, in 1903, acting upon the recommendations of the park commissioners, the city council invited John C. Olmsted to visit Seattle and design a system of parks and boulevards. A landscape architect from Brookline, Massachusetts, John C. Olmsted was a son of Frederick Law Olmsted and was by this time well known in his own right throughout the United States. After coming to Seattle several times, Olmsted prepared a plan quite similar to Schwagerl's earlier one. Olmsted's plan consisted of a boulevard system twenty-four miles long linking parks throughout Seattle. The boulevard would extend along Lake Washington from the city limits on the south to the grounds of the University of Washington on the north, joining the Bailey Peninsula (now Seward Park), Madrona Park, and Washington Park. From the university, the boulevard would turn inland to link Ravenna Park, Green Lake, Woodland Park, and the Fort Lawton Reservation with Smith's Cove on Elliot Bay. Subsidiary boulevards would join yet other parks to the system, which would encircle much of Seattle.[9]

Seattleites responded favorably to Olmsted's plan. In October 1903, the city council officially adopted it, and between 1906 and 1912 bond issues totaling $4 million to implement the plan won public approval. By 1913 much of Olmsted's scheme had been put in force. Twenty-five parks, twelve playgrounds, and twenty-five miles of boulevards lay within Seattle's boundaries.[10]

Several reasons accounted for the success of Olmsted's plan for Seattle. Many Seattleites simply desired to live in a beautiful city with improved recreational facilities. Economic factors also spurred the swift implementation of Olmsted's plan. By the early 1900s, Seattle had recovered from the hard times of the 1890s and was in a period of rapid economic growth. As a consequence, its citizens could better afford the costs of developing a park and boulevard system. Businessmen in particular came to view parks as an investment that would attract settlers and businesses to their city, thus ensuring Seattle's future growth. Social factors also help explain the favorable votes of some Seattleites. Olmsted called for the building of playgrounds in working-class areas as a way of bringing vaguely defined citizenship values to their residents. Middle-class professionals joined businessmen in praising his proposal for the playgrounds as "nurseries of good citizenship" and "cradles of democracy" in which children of all backgrounds could mix and grow into "beautiful manhood and womanhood."[11]

Two business-dominated groups were especially important in backing the park movement. Like many reformers in the Progressive Era across the nation, members of those groups believed that by changing their environments, the character of people could be altered for the better. The Seattle Recreation and Playgrounds League was one such group. Middle-class businessmen and professionals, many of whom were active in political reform movements in Seattle formed the organization in 1912. They argued that parks and playgrounds should be supported as a way "to encourage and foster all recreation and play which will add to the health, happiness and moral uplift of our people" while at the same time "discouraging and aiding in surpressing those amusements which tend to deprave."[12] The Seattle Playgrounds Association, a similar organization established four years earlier, called for more parks and playgrounds because of "the known effects of play upon normal growth and health, as a preventive of crime, as cheaper in dollars and cents than their alternatives—jails, police, and hospitals—and as a Citizen Maker through the ideals of fair play and social cooperation inculcated under the stress of action in organized games of the playground."[13]

Given the varied motives for support, it is not surprising to find that all of the park and boulevard bond issues passed by two-to-one majorities. Of more interest is that while the issues did particularly well in middle-class suburbs, they faced rougher handling in blue-collar wards. The Ballard and Wallingford districts, for instance, often gave them only close favorable votes or actually defeated them. The workingmen living there could see little immediate advantage in the creation of an elaborate and expensive park and boulevard system and may have objected to the implications of social influence inherent in the scheme.[14]

Even as his park and boulevard plans were meeting with success at the polls, John Olmsted was called to Seattle to plan a new campus for the University of Washington. In mid-1903 he was asked to take charge of "the improvement of the large university campus in harmony with the proposed system of parks."[15] Olmsted's campus plan, drawn up over the next two years, stressed the need for comprehensive preparations. Olmsted decried the tendency of university officials to follow a "hand-to-mouth policy" of piecemeal building and called upon them to follow a "comprehensive, systematic and well-organized arrangement of numerous buildings . . . embodying certain general principles and ideas." Specifically, he wanted the erection of "imposing and monumental" buildings on an "important and imposing site" and the replacement of native evergreen trees with deciduous ones, because he thought that wild evergreens would be "incongruous with the formal buildings." Connecting the buildings of the campus to each other and to Seattle's park and boulevard system would be a symmetrical pattern of walks. Linking the campus to Seattle via parkways would, Olmsted hoped, elevate the tone of student life by ensuring "direct communication with the greater part of the existing and future residential districts of the better class of the city."[16]

It was on the campus grounds that Seattle's business and political leaders sponsored a world's fair, the Alaska-Yukon-Pacific Exposition, in the summer of 1909. The inspiration for this exposition came initially from a group of Alaska's gold-rush pioneers who desired to establish an Alaskan exhibit in Seattle, which they did in 1905. Support for something larger began in 1906, when fifty

Seattle businessmen, mostly merchants, formed an exhibition company. The company sponsored the fair three years later. Business leaders viewed the Alaska-Yukon-Pacific Exposition as a major advertisement for their city, a lure to attract capital, industry, and commerce from around the nation.[17]

As in the case of park development, more was involved in the exposition than economics, however. Like Olmsted's plans for parks and boulevards and the new university campus, the fair served as a model for planning. The exposition company hired the Olmsted Brothers firm to design the fairgrounds. Showing more sensitivity to the natural environment than he had in his plans for the university campus, John Olmsted produced a plan that took advantage of its natural setting. He oriented the central portion of the grounds and buildings along a major axis that opened onto a vista of Mount Rainier. Secondary axes provided views of Lake Union and Lake Washington.[18] Nearly four million people came to the exposition, and the fair left many with a sense that planning could improve their environment. At the conclusion of the exposition, the Seattle Chamber of Commerce called for the construction of a Museum of Arts and Sciences as "a natural outgrowth of the exposition" and urged the creation of a Fine Arts Association to work for civic improvements in Seattle. The chamber also persuaded the city council to allocate funds for the preservation of the beauty of the fairgrounds and for their integration into Seattle's park system.[19]

The Municipal Plans Commission

The park and exposition campaigns led some Seattleites to begin thinking of additional ways to improve their city. In the early 1900s, the Washington State Chapter of the American Institute of Architects (WSCAIA) took its first steps to promote civic improvements. Composed mainly of Seattle architects, the WSCAIA had been formed in 1894 and acted as a catalyst in the emerging campaign to improve Seattle. In the opening years of the twentieth century, the WSCAIA sponsored an exhibit demonstrating advances being made in city planning in Washington, D.C., prepared revisions to the city's building ordinances, and worked with business groups to promote their products throughout the Pacific Northwest.[20] Civic pride lay behind many of the activities. For instance, in early 1907 the WSCAIA joined with the Seattle Manufacturers' Association to call for the construction of a new city hall because "the needs of the City of Seattle demand the construction of a City Hall worthy of the city."[21]

From those beginnings, the WSCAIA moved on to propose revisions to Seattle's city charter creating an office of the superintendent of buildings separate from the city's board of public works and the formation of a commission composed of professional architects and builders to advise the city council on "matters pertaining to municipal improvements which involve artistic consideration." In making those proposals, the WSCAIA cooperated closely with business groups in Seattle—the Chamber of Commerce, the Manufacturers' Association, and the Commercial Club—and with labor organizations, the Building Trades Assembly, and the Master Builders Association.[22] Backed by Seattle's newspapers as a way "to meet the progressive needs of a growing city," the proposals easily won approval by large margins at a city election in 1908.[23]

Spurred on by their success, in January 1909 members of the WSCAIA conferred with representatives of improvement clubs and with members of the Pacific Northwest Society of Engineers, a well-established organization of building engineers and architects. In the words of Charles Bebb, the president of the WSCAIA, they discussed "ways and means for procuring a comprehensive plan for the future development along civic lines of the City of Seattle." Noting that Washington, D.C., Cleveland, Boston, San Francisco, Los Angeles, and other cities across the nation had become deeply involved in planning, Bebb argued that Seattle had to follow suite or fall behind its more progressive counterparts. The time to begin, he thought, was now. Seattle was still young enough to accomplish a great deal. Seattle was not as built up, as fully developed, as most eastern cities and thus offered more scope to planners. Planning was needed, Bebb argued, "so that the future development of the city shall not be left to haphazard and chance growth and that the public may be assured that all the money that will normally be spent each year for improvements will be spent with farsighted wisdom." The scheme would not be "new or visionary," he stressed, but "a practical reality" similar to what was being adopted in cities across the nation. From that meeting came the formation of a Municipal Plans League one month later.[24]

The Municipal Plans League spearheaded the growing planning campaign in Seattle. The league called for the preparation of a city plan encompassing street and transportation improvements, new harbor facilities, the construction of a civic center, and further work on parks and boulevards for Seattle.[25] In the fall of 1909, league members held several meetings with members of business groups. Finally, in late November the Municipal Plans League, the WSCAIA, the Chamber of Commerce, and the Commercial Club jointly endorsed a resolution drafted by architect Carl Gould, who belonged to the WSCAIA, served on the executive committee of the league, and had worked with Daniel Burnham on his plan for San Francisco. The resolution called on the city council to place before the voters a city charter amendment setting up a commission of three experts to draft a plan for Seattle. They were to be advised by twenty-one Seattleites representing the city's business and labor organizations. The city council agreed to the request.[26] Having achieved unity of purpose among themselves, Seattle's architectural and business organizations next had to convince their city's voters of the need for city planning.

Planning proponents emphasized economic arguments in seeking approval for a Municipal Plans Commission. In the words of George Walker, a lawyer deeply involved in the campaign, planning, far from being expensive, meant simply "taking things as we find them and planning wisely, conservatively, and economically." Moreover, noted Walker, "there is competition among cities just as there is in other lines . . . the city that is up-to-date and modern leads . . . others fall behind."[27] As Walker's arguments suggest, perceptions of urban rivalry played a significant role in motivating those favoring planning in Seattle. Members of the WSCAIA urged the establishment of a planning commission in part because "the City of Portland is moving to the same end and there is the possibility of our suffering the chagrin of seeing a smaller city occupy our natural position of the leading city of the Northwest."[28] W. Marbury Somervell, a leading Seattle architect, summarized many of the economic reasons put forward in support of planning:

It is not enough to tell the taxpayer that he should have a more beautiful city, but to show him conclusively that beauty and hygiene, and all that goes to make a city useful and attractive, mean simply unity of purpose . . . Visitors are impressed; and the municipality is advertised; trade is attracted by the increase in population and more amenable conditions of life; values quickly increase with better trade, and at the same time the [tax] rates are kept at a lower level.[29]

Social and moral factors also influenced advocates of planning. Gould hoped that planning would promote "the cause of civic unity."[30] The Reverend Mark Mathews, a well-known Protestant minister and a fiery advocate of moral reform in city politics, may have had the same thing in mind when he called for the establishment of the planning commission because "the improvements of the city ought to have in view the whole city, and the city ought to be developed as a whole."[31] Similarly, the Seattle *Post-Intelligencer*, a leading newspaper, backed the creation of a planning commission so that "Seattle may grow along definite and harmonious lines."[32]

Business and labor organizations jointly backed the proposal. Members of the Chamber of Commerce and the Commercial Club pushed for it, observing that "the plans are not necessarily for immediate fulfillment, but are to serve as a guide for years to come."[33] Numerous neighborhood improvement clubs, now linked in the Federated Improvement Clubs, came out for it. The Workingmen's League, a body of unionized workers formed to support labor candidates for city offices, pressed for the measure "to create a better understanding in the minds of the public as to the future development of a great city." The president of the Seattle Central Labor Council urged workers to stand "shoulder to shoulder" with their city's business organizations in backing the measure.[34] Important political support came from R. H. Thomson, Seattle's city engineer. Thomson had won local acclaim for reshaping Seattle by lowering its hills, which had stood as formidable barriers to the city's expansion. As Thomson later noted, "I put in a great deal of labor in securing this Municipal Plans Commission."[35]

Favored by a broad spectrum of business, professional, and labor organizations and facing no organized opposition, the city charter amendment setting up a Municipal Plans Commission won a resounding victory at the polls, passing by a margin of 13,852 to 7,371 votes.[36] At that time, nearly all Seattleites could agree that city planning could be beneficial. Inspired by the development of their parks and boulevards and by what they had recently seen at the Alaska-Yukon-Pacific Exposition, they hoped to create an improved urban environment.

A strong progressive movement was developing in city politics, and city planning became loosely associated with progressivism.[37] In Seattle progressivism came to revolve around two major clusters of issues: first, whether Seattle should have a "moral" government embodying values of hard work, temperance, and the abolition of vice and, second, whether the city's public utilities, including street railroads, should be municipally owned. The twin issues of moral reform and municipal ownership merged in 1911 when the city's mayor, Hiram Gill, was recalled from office. Gill had championed Seattle as a "wide-open" town, even to the extent of directly involving the city government and city funds in the building of a gigantic house of prostitution. At Gill's direction, the city council rerouted streets and granted a franchise to a new street railroad line to serve the bordello. Like members of San Francisco's Union Labor party, Gill and city councilmen associated with him were also suspected of taking numerous bribes from private street railroads and other utility companies in return for giving them franchises.

To combat "Gillism," a group of middle-class businessmen formed the Public Welfare League at a meeting sponsored by the Commercial Club in 1910. The members thought Gill's actions were creating an unsavory national image for Seattle and that that image was retarding economic growth by scaring away businessmen and capital that might otherwise move to Seattle. Gill was, one of the league's petitions claimed, "a menace to the business enterprises and moral welfare" of Seattle.[38] Gill badly misjudged the changing desires of most of Seattle's businessmen. In an address to the Chamber of Commerce in April 1910, he discussed what he viewed as the proper relationship between government and business:

I recognize, first and foremost, that men are in business with one primary aim, to make money. They are not running their

businesses to display pretty show windows, keep their side-
walk clean, or improve the ethical tone of the community.
Their primary object is to get the dollar into the cash register, and because it is the businessmen who make the prosperity of the city, I believe the city government should do all
in its power to help the businessmen get the money. . . . A
"City Beautiful" will be encouraged so long as it is a "City
Practical" and a "City Economical."[39]

Such appeals, which had been persuasive in earlier times, no
longer sufficed. Seattle was no longer a frontier outpost, and its
business leaders wanted national recognition and continued
growth for their city. Gill was an anachronism who would have to
go. In a hotly contested election in 1911 the league succeeded in
removing Gill from office by convincing many of Seattle's prosperous workers, as well as the city's burgeoning groups of middle-
class businessmen and professionals, to vote against him. Only
less-prosperous, downtown workers and the business leaders who
benefited directly from Gill's political favors supported him. This
was the zenith of progressivism.

As in San Francisco, Oakland, and Los Angeles, city planning
became partially linked to progressivism in Seattle. Many of the
same people, especially middle-class businessmen, supported
both movements. Many of those joining the Public Welfare
League and an earlier reform group, the Municipal Ownership
Party (established in 1905), were also active in the Municipal
Plans League, which pressed so strongly for the creation of the
Municipal Plans Commission. Moreover, many of those same
Seattleites became members of the Municipal League, a body of
middle-class businessmen and professionals organized in 1910 to
work for a broad spectrum of progressive reforms in the city
government.[40] Businessmen supported reform politics and city
planning for many of the same reasons. They wanted to improve
Seattle's image nationally and on the Pacific Coast, thus allowing
Seattle to attract new immigrants, business firms, and capital.
Moral and social issues also ran through both movements. By
closing down Seattle's "restricted area" of saloons and gambling
houses, and by backing city planning measures, many Seattleites, again especially middle-class businessmen, hoped to

create a homogeneous society open to their values and way of life.

Shortly after Seattle's 1910 municipal elections, at about the same time that the campaign to recall Gill was beginning, the Municipal Plans Commission took form. As stipulated by the city charter amendment, the commission consisted of twenty-one members: three city councilmen, the city engineer Thomson, a representative of the King County commissioners, a member of the board of education, a member of the park board, and fourteen citizens chosen by business, labor, and architectural organizations. The fourteen citizens included representatives from the Chamber of Commerce, the Manufacturers' Association, the Commercial Club, the Seattle Real Estate Association, the Waterfront Owners, the Steam Railway Companies, the Seattle Clearing House Association, the Central Labor Council, the Carpenters Union, the WSCAIA, and the Pacific Society of Civil Engineers.[41]

Unlike the situation in San Francisco where the AAISF operated separately and independently from the city government, the Municipal Plans Commission was, by the city charter amendment, part of the city government in Seattle, if only for a limited time. Although differing in their official roles, the two organizations were similar in their functions. Both were only advisory; neither could mandate actions for their city governments to follow. Before being put into practice, their recommendations had to be approved in city elections. Businessmen, especially merchants, were active participants in both bodies, for through them they hoped to work out their planning desires.

The Municipal Plans Commission moved quickly to select the three experts who would undertake the actual planning. A committee composed of Thomson, C. J. Smith of the Chamber of Commerce, and Frank Mullen of the city council initially considered five planners, landscape architects, and engineers. Disregarding its original charge to choose three experts jointly to prepare a plan for Seattle, the committee picked Virgil Bogue to assume command of the preparation of the entire city plan by himself. Bogue had been contacted initially to undertake only the planning of new streets and harbor facilities. He accepted the position in September, 1910 in return for a salary of $1,500 per month.[42]

The Bogue Plan for Seattle

Bogue was particularly well qualified for the engineering tasks at hand. A graduate of the Rensselaer Polytechnic Institute, Bogue had worked briefly for F. L. Olmsted, Sr. He had then gone on to design a route for the first railroad to cross the Andes and had located the Northern Pacific Railroad's route through the Cascade Mountains just east of Seattle. Perhaps most significantly, Bogue had, as a consulting engineer to the King County Board of Tideland Appraisers, drafted a plan for the development of Seattle's harbor in 1895. Although sixty-four years old in 1910, Bogue was full of life and eager to accept new challenges.[43]

Bogue probably owed his choice to Thomson, Seattle's city engineer. Both men had the same mentality. Thomson was an engineer with little feeling for Seattle's topography. Rather than work with them, Thomson preferred to level Seattle's hills by using hydraulic cannons to wash them into Puget Sound. As the historian William Wilson has observed, "Thomson's sympathy with the natural environment was limited to allowing water to run downhill."[44] Bogue thought in the same way; and it is no surprise that, while the report he ultimately drafted was in some repects an engineering marvel, it took little account of the topography of Seattle's natural features. Although most Seattleites were pleased with the choice of Bogue, not all were. The members of the WSCAIA initially felt a sense of betrayal, for Bogue was too much of an engineer and not enough of a planner for their tastes.[45] Perhaps because of such feelings John Olmsted was retained, after further negotiations, as a consultant to advise Bogue on parks and boulevards.[46]

Bogue came to Seattle to begin his work in September 1910. Upon his arrival, Bogue emphasized that planning would foster Seattle's growth in the most economical way by eliminating waste in general and by aiding in meshing the city's street system with its harbor facilities in particular. True to his engineering background, Bogue was especially happy to find that Thomson's work in regrading hills and laying out new streets could be incorporated directly into his planning ideas.[47]

The actual work of preparing the city plan proceeded rapidly, given the magnitude of the task. Assisted by a few close subordinates, Bogue was in overall charge of the planning effort. However, the twenty-one-member Municipal Plans Commission, now divided into committees dealing with specific topics, remained important. Both Bogue and the commission also frequently conferred with the WSCAIA, the Pacific Northwest Society of Engineers, the Chamber of Commerce, and other business and professional bodies. Private citizens—Joseph Blethen, the editor of the Seattle *Times*, Edmund Meany, a well-known professor of history at the University of Washington, and George and C. A. Kinnear, prominent real estate men with interests in the southern end of the downtown district—also received hearings from committees of the commission. After the appropriate committee of the Municipal Plans Commission dealt with a particular topic, the matter was referred to the commission as a whole and to Bogue to ensure that specific decisions would fit into the plan Bogue was drafting for the city. Considerable local input from organized groups went into the preparation of the Bogue Plan, in marked contrast to the way the Burnham Plan was prepared for San Francisco.[48]

Central to the Bogue Plan were transportation improvements. Most important was the creation of a system of arterial highways and radial streets, adjusted only slightly for Seattle's hilly topography, to speed the flow of traffic around Seattle's congested business district and to connect a proposed civic center with the rest of the city. A new Central Avenue would form a north-south axis for Seattle's revised street system. It would extend from the established downtown district to the civic center just southwest of Lake Union, then continue along the west shore of Lake Union and run in a northerly direction past Green Lake to the county line. Numerous tunnels would slice through Seattle's hills to facilitate traffic movement between previously separated parts of the city. The plan also made detailed recommendations for the location of steam railroad lines, including the construction of a new union passenger station several blocks north of the proposed civic center, the construction of a ninety-one-mile-long rapid transit system, and the extension of interurban and ferry service to link Seattle to its surrounding area. It included recommendations for electric street railroads to connect Seattle's increasingly dispersed neighborhoods with its downtown district, proposed civic center, and waterfront.[49]

Virgil Bogue called for a new union train station. From the Bogue Plan for Seattle.

Harbor improvements also attracted great attention from Bogue and the Municipal Plans Commission. Seven one-thousand-foot piers would turn Harbor Island, at the time undeveloped mudflats at the south end of Seattle's port on Elliot Bay, into a major commercial complex. Two fifteen-hundred-foot piers would add to the importance of Smith's Cove at the northern end of Elliot Bay. In between those complexes two systems of docks—one for ferries and Alaska steamers, the other for Seattle's fleet of small ships plying the waters of Puget Sound—would transform the central waterfront. Lake Union and the southern end of Lake Washington were slated to become industrial areas, while the northern end of Lake Washington was designated a residential and vacation region.[50]

To serve as the focal point for Seattle, Bogue designed a civic center to be located several miles north of the established business district at the intersection of Fourth Avenue and Blanchard Street. The area was just being made accessible by Thomson's leveling of Denny Hill. Bogue believed the site possessed a number of advantages over a downtown location: the availability of relatively cheap land, a location near what he thought would be the future center of Seattle's population, and easy transportation access to the rest of

Virgil Bogue's plan included a new civic center; this view looks south along the proposed Central Avenue. From the Bogue Plan for Seattle.

the city. Bogue called for a six-building center grouped together in an imposing manner and having impressive views of Mount Rainier to the south and the Olympic Mountains to the west.[51]

Finally, the Bogue Plan envisioned a system of parks, boulevards, and municipal ornaments for Seattle and the surrounding region. For the most part, Bogue followed Olmsted's ideas within Seattle's city limits. Outside of Seattle Bogue desired the creation or improvement of twenty-two parks ranging in size from 15 to 475 acres, partially linked by boulevards and parkways. Municipal decorations—concourses, esplanades, the beautification of traffic intersections, and a tall obelisk facing Puget Sound at Duwamish Head—would further enhance Seattle.[52]

Bogue and the members of the Municipal Plans Commission hoped their plan would both foster Seattle's economic growth and unite the city spatially. Improvements in the city's harbor and transportation layouts and the meshing of those two systems would, they anticipated, put Seattle ahead of its urban rivals as the Pacific Coast's commercial and manufacturing center. After noting that Los Angeles, San Diego, San Francisco, and Portland were all planning major harbor and transportation improvements, Bogue warned that unless Seattle responded to those challenges the city would "surely fall behind other competitors for the accumulation of worldwide trade." Speed was essential, Bogue contended, in light of the imminent completion of the Panama Canal. Transportation improvements were needed, not simply for their economic stimulus, but also because they would bring Seattle's rapid spatial expansion under control. The arterial highways and the unified electric street railroad system would, planning advocates thought, tie together Seattle's various neighborhoods.[53]

The civic center and the parks were also intended to be unifying forces. Bogue and the members of the Municipal Plans Commission believed that an impressive civic center would inspire Seattleites with a sense of common purpose very similar to the civic patriotism that James Phelan had hoped planning would bring to San Francisco. At the civic center "large gatherings of citizens" could congregate for "pageants and for the formal reception of delegates from other cities or foreign countries." The civic center would mold personalities along useful paths. After observing that "environment in youth has enormous influence on the personal and civic education of future citizens," Bogue applauded civic centers for their ability to uplift the minds and spirits of urbanites.[54] The same concern for a united populace imbued with common values motivated Bogue's desire for a park and boulevard system. Like John C. Olmsted and his supporters, Bogue declared that parks and playgrounds would instill citizenship values in Seattleites:

The taxpayer now knows by statistics of unquestioned accuracy that the maintenance of places of healthful exercise, amusement, and self-improvement for those who would otherwise pass their formative years in adverse, and possibly degrading circumstances, is more profitable than that of reformatory institutions for children and penitentiaries for adults. . . . At least a three-fold benefit accrues to the public from the development of public playgrounds, viz.: the arrest of disease and vice, a constantly decreasing prison-roll, the preparation of useful, law-abiding citizens. . . . Those who learn to play well will be more apt to work with a purpose.[55]

The Bogue Plan dealt with many facets of Seattle's development; it was much more than simply a scheme for the city's beautification. More of an engineering document than the Burnham Plan for San Francisco or the Robinson plans for Oakland and Los Angeles, the Bogue Plan was particularly detailed in its analysis of the harbor and transportation needs of Seattle. Yet the Bogue Plan had shortcomings. Like most city plans drafted in the Progressive Era, it said little about the housing needs of most people. Moreover, the proposals for transportation improvements rode roughshod over Seattle's hilly terrain and would soon be made partially obsolete by the widespread adoption of the automobile.

The Fight for the Bogue Plan

Bogue presented his completed plan to the Municipal Plans Commission for that body's final approval in August 1911. With only three negative votes—cast by members representing the city council and the county commissioners, who may have been worried about the cost of implementing Bogue's ideas—the commission accepted the Bogue Plan. The commission then submitted the plan to the city council with the request that it be embodied in a city charter amendment for public ratification in the March 1912 city election. Should the charter amendment pass, city officials would be required to follow the Bogue Plan as a mandatory guide in laying out the future development of Seattle. The city council agreed to place the Bogue Plan on the ballot. With its work seemingly complete, the Municipal Plans Commission disbanded in late 1911.[56]

Many business, professional, and labor bodies found immediate praise for the Bogue Plan. The secretary of the Chamber of Commerce observed that "the great cities of the future will not be creatures of chance. Early preparations will smooth the way and hasten their advancement." Bogue's ideas, he concluded, represented "excellent progress" particularly because "Bogue has always kept in mind the minimizing of expense . . . so as not to saddle the community with an unwieldy burden."[57] Members of the WSCAIA, who had harbored doubts about Bogue, now applauded his "sincere appreciation of the needs for a comprehensive plan" and elected him as an honorary member of their organization.[58] Thomson, Bogue's initial sponsor, called his work "most excellent."[59] The Seattle Central Labor Council, the powerful clearinghouse for Seattle's strong craft unions, commended the plan and allocated a small sum to help publicize it.[60] Nonetheless, opposition to the work of Bogue and the Municipal Plans Commission materialized even as the Bogue Plan was being prepared. Although planning advocates were able to defeat the early threats to their ideas, this opposition boded ill for the adoption of the Bogue Plan.

Most serious were challenges from businessmen desiring to have Seattle build a new city hall at the south end of the city's established business district rather than to the north as specified in the Bogue Plan. By 1910 the city government had outgrown its old headquarters. The city council placed on the ballot—the same one that presented the proposal for a Municipal Plans Commission to Seattleites—a bond issue to purchase land for a new city hall site at Third Avenue and Yesler Way at the southern end of Seattle's downtown district. Those favoring the adoption of the Bogue Plan quickly rallied to oppose the bond issue.[61]

The campaigns for and against the bonds to buy land for a new city hall sorely divided Seattle's business community. On one level, the issue developed into a struggle between businessmen with real estate interests in the southern section of Seattle's downtown district and businessmen in other parts of the city. Those with property downtown desired the immediate construction of the city hall near their properties as a way of increasing their real estate values. Businessmen elsewhere in the city favored waiting until the Bogue Plan incorporating a new city hall as part of a civic center was drafted before reaching any decision. At a second level, the bond issue began dividing Seattle business leaders into those favoring a dense downtown of skyscrapers like New York (the southern downtown area was already heavily constructed and could only grow up) and those who favored a more dispersed downtown area, with the city hall in a new part of town.[62]

Poorly defined, those issues were only just emerging in 1910. While the Chamber of Commerce backed the proposal for the Municipal Plans Commission, it also supported the proposal to buy land for a city hall in the established downtown area. The bonds passed by a vote of 11,975 to 7,108.[63] (Seattle's bonds required only a simple majority favorable vote to go into effect.) Following up on their initial success, the south-end businessmen worked to win public approval for additional bonds to build the city hall on the land just purchased. However, opposition from the Municipal Plans Commission, the Municipal League, and some fifty improvement clubs and church groups defeated the proposed bonds in late 1910.[64] A renewed attempt to commit Seattleites to a southern location for the city hall met the same fate in 1911. As Charles Allen, an architect who headed the City Plan Committee of the Municipal League, explained, the bonds "would jeopardize the integrity of the Bogue Plan" and should be killed. Members of the Municipal League, working with Seattle's Ministerial Federation, an organization of Protestant churches, mounted a massive campaign against the bonds. They advertised in Seattle's newspapers, distributed pamphlets denouncing the bonds, and spoke against them at numerous public meetings.[65] Such opposition, combined with a willingness on the part of most Seattleites to wait and see what the Bogue Plan entailed, defeated the bonds.[66]

With the conclusion of the votes on the city hall bond issues, the battle lines over city planning were drawn. Those favoring the Bogue Plan had demonstrated an ability to organize and turn back efforts to subvert it. They had not, however, yet shown an ability to win public approval for their specific planning ideas. The contests over the locations of the city hall were simply preliminaries to the main fight over the acceptance of the Bogue Plan as a guide for Seattle's growth.

Planning advocates initiated their campaign for public approval of the Bogue Plan during the late summer and fall of 1911, with the Municipal League leading the fight. The league's members spoke at meetings of local improvement clubs and sponsored mass rallies to publicize the plan. The organization financed the printing and distribution of ten thousand copies of the plan and took out advertisements in Seattle's newspapers in support of the Bogue Plan. The WSCAIA worked closely with the Municipal League in providing lecturers for groups that wanted to learn about the plan and set up exhibits about it at libraries and other public places. Additional professional and business organizations, most notably the Commercial Club and the Pacific Northwest Society of Civil Engineers, worked for the plan.[67]

Those favoring adoption of the Bogue Plan stressed its anticipated economic benefits. They repeatedly argued that planning would decrease the cost of providing public utilities and services for Seattle, thus helping keep taxes low. In a well-worn claim, they asserted that a planned city, in addition to being a functionally integrated city, would also be a beautiful city; and they saw beauty as having a definite economic value in attracting visitors and new residents to Seattle.[68]

The transportation and harbor improvements of the Bogue Plan won special praise as bound to spur economic growth. With the completion of the Panama Canal approaching, Seattle's planning advocates, like those in San Francisco, claimed that it was necessary to rearrange their city's port facilities and internal transportation network to handle the expected increase in trade. Failure to do so would, they warned, entail the risk of having that commerce travel through the harbors of Seattle's rivals, San Francisco and Portland. "Other cities on the Pacific Coast are spending millions to attract the commerce incident to the opening of the Panama Canal," reported the City Plans Committee of the Municipal League. "What chance has Seattle in competition if it does not plan for the proper utilization of its natural advantages as a seaport?"[69]

A flyer widely distributed by the Municipal League during the closing days of the campaign summarized the perceived economic advantages of planning:

What the plan means:
1. Economy in transportation. We probably lose today $500,000 a year in hauling freight over heavy grades—that is, we lose interest on an investment of over $8,000,000.

2. The saving of the wasteful practice of doing work over again when once done. . . .

3. Prevention of high rents in a monopolized business area. High rents increase the cost of goods to the people.

4. Prevention of congestion of business and traffic with its great loss in time and money to the travelling public and carriers of freight.

5. Taking the direction of the city's growth out of the hands of real estate speculators and putting it in the hands of the people.

6. The most efficient development of the harbor and the provision of factory sites . . .

7. The opening of Seattle to access by new railroads.

8. Decreasing the ultimate cost of necessary work by proceeding in a systematic manner instead of haphazard.

9. The making of a city beautiful as well as a city useful. As an advertisement alone the adoption of the plan would pay for itself many times.[70]

While economic arguments dominated the presentations of those working for the Bogue Plan, social considerations were also important. Thomson, the powerful city engineer, lent his support because he thought the plan was needed "to produce a sanitary city" and to "so arrange the streets and parks of the city that there shall be the best opportunities afforded for light and air and the best opportunities afforded for the laborer to come quickly from his home to the places of recreation." Thomson also found praise for the civic center for bringing "culture and refinement" to workingmen.[71] The City Plans Committee of the Municipal League anticipated that the plan would promote the cause of civic unity because it would "harmonize the conflict of purposes" and secure for the people "conditions adapted to the maximum of productive efficiency, of health and enjoyment of life."[72]

Undergirding many of the arguments in favor of the Bogue Plan was the issue of civic pride, a desire on the part of planning proponents to see Seattle recognized as the premier metropolis of the Pacific Coast and as a leading national center. In an advertisement placed in Seattle's leading newspapers, members of the Municipal League noted that planning advocates in Portland were "united toward making that city the tourist headquarters and convention city of the Northwest as well as making it as attractive as possible for its permanent residents." They urged Seattleites to counter those actions by working "along the lines of public spirit, common sense, and progress."[73] Similarly, they observed that San Francisco's Board of Supervisers was supporting the building of a new city hall and argued that Seattle's officials should do no less.[74] By the same token, an editorial in the *Town Crier* noted that, should the Bogue Plan be implemented, "we would become the talk of the country as having the most beautiful and useful civic center in the world" and concluded that "the value of this as an advertisement will alone be worth more than the cost of the ground and the buildings."[75] The secretary of the Municipal League perhaps best summarized that type of sentiment when he called for a favorable vote for the Bogue Plan, because "no obstacles should be allowed at this time to cast their shadow before a city with a future, the brightest of all, on the Pacific Coast."[76]

Businessmen owning property in the south end of Seattle's downtown district mounted the most vocal and best organized opposition to the plan. Their opposition reached a climax with the formation in February 1912 of a Civic Plans Investigation Committee. The committee issued a widely read pamphlet that attacked the Bogue Plan as too expensive, impractical, and inflexible. In particular, the committee opposed the plan for placing the civic center north of the established business area. To do so would, its members claimed, upset the flow of business transactions and impede Seattle's economic growth. As in the past, they pressed for the building of a new city hall on the land the city already owned in the southern section of Seattle's established business district at Third Avenue and Yesler Way.[77]

While downtown businessmen rallied most strongly against the Bogue Plan, other groups and individuals opposed it as well. George Cotterill—a well-known engineer who had worked on the Alaska-Yukon-Pacific Exposition and who ran successfully as a reform candidate for mayor in 1912—had long supported the idea of city planning but now came out against the plan as too rigid and costly.[78] In fact, considerable opposition developed among Seattleites along the lines that the Bogue Plan, as a mandatory guide for civic improvements, would prove inflexible and expensive. Representatives of organized labor opposed the plan in part for

Virgil Bogue's proposed civic center would have been constructed in a new section of Seattle. From the Bogue Plan for Seattle.

those reasons. The leaders of the Central Labor Council urged its members to vote against the plan. They believed it might prove be too difficult to alter in the future and they thought that the park and boulevard system should be developed separately from the plan.[79]

Some business organizations that had earlier favored the Bogue Plan saw less need for it in 1912. Of great importance in that regard were efforts to develop Seattle's harbor.[80] Intercity rivalry was of utmost significance. Perceiving that "it is useless to hope for great results from the opening of the Panama Canal unless the harbor is large," members of the Portland Chamber of Commerce secured passage for a city charter amendment creating a Portland Commission of Public Docks in 1910.[81] Authorized to sell up to $2.5 million in bonds, the commission opened the city's first publicly owned docks for business in 1914 and 1915. Seattle's business leaders were awakened by the challenge. "San Francisco, Los Angeles, San Diego, and Portland are spending millions of dollars in harbor improvements," argued Seattle merchants. "Seattle must meet this competition."[82] The Chamber of Commerce, Commercial Club, and numerous neighborhood improvement clubs responded by successfully pushing for the passage of a $2.275 million harbor bond issue in late 1910. During the next two years those organizations won approval for the establishment of a Seattle Port Commission to develop their city's harbor, together with additional bonds recommended by the new commission to build up the harbor.[83] The establishment of the Port Commission and the passage of the bond issues seemed to negate the need for the harbor proposals in the Bogue Plan.

Bereft of much of its former support and opposed by powerful individuals and organizations, the Bogue Plan went down to a crushing defeat at the polls. The final tally at the March 1912 election was 24,966 votes against the plan, with only 14,506 in favor of it. In none of Seattle's fourteen wards did the plan receive a favorable vote.[84] As the vote favoring the establishment of the Municipal Plans Commission in 1910 had shown, most Seattleites approved of the general idea of city planning; but many of those same people voted against the Bogue Plan when they came to view it as threatening their specific interests. Downtown businessmen disliked the proposal to place the civic center in a newly developing area to the north, and other businessmen came to see the plan's harbor proposals as irrelevant or redundant. Labor leaders objected to some of the specifics of the plan.

Equally important was the feeling on the part of many that the plan was simply too rigid. The mandatory nature of the Bogue Plan set it apart from most city plans of the period, which were only advisory. Some members of the Municipal League—for instance, Carl Gould, who had watched the piecemeal defeat of the Burnham Plan in San Francisco—liked the mandatory feature of the Bogue Plan. Most Seattleites did not. They thought that aspect of the plan would deprive the city government of the ability to change with the times in planning for the future.[85]

The matter of expense also troubled Seattleites. Planning advocates argued in vain that building a planned city would in the long run be less expensive than constructing an unplanned one. Typical of the many who called for the defeat of the Bogue Plan was one opponent who decided to vote against it because "Seattle has more immediate needs that should have the support of her energy and of her tax and bond paying powers. Let us have payrolls and health [a reference to the need for better water and sewer systems] now—luxury and art as we can afford them."[86] Writing in the same vein was a Minnie Frazier, who described herself and her husband as "Independent, Non-Partisan, Insurgent Radicals." As she explained to Joe Smith, a reformist newspaperman and politician, "We shall vote *No* on Bogue Plans. *No* on Park Bonds. Luxuries can wait while necessities are lacking."[87]

Their position was understandable. As a result of the efforts being made to regrade Seattle's hills, put in new water and sewer lines, and build parks, Seattleites were heavily taxed. By 1915 Seattle trailed only San Francisco of all the major cities in the United States in terms of per capita revenue receipts and outlays.[88]

In a sense, the defeat of the Bogue Plan mirrored the collapse of Seattle's progressive movement. Just as most Seattleites could agree that city planning in the abstract was a good idea, only to vote against it when presented with a concrete planning proposal, so, too, did many Seattleites defect from the progressive campaign when presented with specific proposals that threatened to injure their individual interests. New issues arose after 1911 to drive a wedge between the properous workers and the middle-class businessmen and professionals, and by the First World War the city's reform coalition had shattered and progressivism had died. In fact, Hiram Gill, who had been recalled from office in 1911, championed the cause of organized labor to win a stunning reelection as Seattle's mayor in 1914.[89]

Later Planning Efforts

City planning and improvement efforts continued in Seattle after the defeat of the Bogue Plan but in less comprehensive forms. While some public attempts at planning continued, private work increased in importance. Moreover, whether public or private, the efforts became more limited in scope. The idea of overall city planning quickly eroded.

No sooner had the Bogue Plan been defeated than the struggle over where to build a city hall was renewed. Opposing groups succeeded in having the city council place two very different measures on the ballot in the fall of 1912. Businessmen from the south end of the downtown district pushed a proposal for a $950,000 municipal building-county courthouse at Third and Yesler. Members of the WSCAIA and the Municipal League countered with a proposition for a similar structure costing $1.4 million at the more northerly location designated in the Bogue Plan. The south-end businessmen formed a Public Buildings Improvement Association to press for their location as the most economical and convenient. "The city needs factories and payrolls," the head of the organization argued, "and factories do not come to cities which waste their money and overtax their people." He concluded, "It is not classical art that has made for the greatness of the United States, it is commerce and industry."[90]

Those backing the northern location formed a Civic Center Association and responded by drawing a more positive connection between art and trade. One member of the Municipal League and the Civic Center Association observed, "I believe a few beautiful buildings grouped together would do more than any other single factor in attracting to Seattle the population which is now on the eve of moving to the Pacific Coast."[91] Urging the passage of bonds for a city hall at the northern site, a leading member of the Chamber of Commerce noted that Seattle had recently lost a proposed Ford Motors assembly plant to Portland and predicted that "if Seattle will not plan ahead . . . she will lose out in scores of similiar cases."[92] Nonetheless, those favoring the northern location were on the defensive after the defeat of the Bogue Plan and proved unconvincing to most Seattleites. The southern site was chosen, and construction of the municipal building-courthouse was finished at that location in 1916.[93]

The final act of Seattle's prewar public city planning drama was played out in 1914. In that year the Municipal League spearheaded a drive to have the city build a large civic auditorium similar to the one being constructed in Oakland. Proponents of the auditorium claimed that it would place Seattle ahead of other Pacific Coast cities in attracting visitors and settlers and that it would help unite Seattle socially by providing an arena in which massive civic celebrations could be staged. By 1914 Seattle was in the grips of a recession, however. Most Seattleites, even some members of the Municipal League, thought that the proposed auditorium was an unnecessary luxury and defeated the proposal for it at the polls.[94]

With their failure to secure adequate backing for their public proposals, planning advocates explored private spheres of endeavor. During the summer of 1912, the Seattle Garden Club, the Real Estate Association, and local improvement clubs mounted a drive to clean up Seattle's vacant lots and plant them with vegetables. At ceremonies inaugurating the campaign, Mayor George Dilling and Mayor-elect Cotterill spoke favorably of the movement, and the president of the Garden Club drove his team of blooded horses at the plow. The Municipal League soon became involved in the campaign because, as one member explained, "it is not just for respectable people to be obliged to live next to a human pig-sty." The movement waxed and waned over the next few years until the Garden Club ended its active sponsorship in 1916, noting with satisfaction that "indications of the activity of the club are apparent throughout the city."[95] Suggesting new directions that planning would take in the future—a growing concern with social conditions—the Municipal League also cooperated with the WSCAIA and the Seattle Central Council of Social Agencies in trying to improve the quality of life for Seattleites through various private associations.[96]

By far the most comprehensive building actions involved the University of Washington. In 1861 the university had received ten acres of what would become the heart of Seattle's business district as a gift; and for years the university was located on that tract. However, as the surrounding area became settled and developed, the university moved in 1894–95 to a new site. Its present location is on Lake Washington several miles to the northeast, where the Alaska-Yukon-Pacific Exposition was held. The move left the university with the question of what to do with its downtown lands. The university chose to keep and develop the property as a source of rental income. Throughout the Progressive Era, the university's board of trustees worked with a private company, the Metropolitan Building Company, to develop the university lands as a single unit. A number of skyscrapers, most notably the White-Henry-Stuart Building, went up on the land.[97]

The coming of World War I halted attempts at comprehensive city planning in Seattle. When planning was revived with the creation of a City Planning Commission by the city council in 1924, the methods and goals of planners differed from those of the prewar years. Planners in Seattle, as was true of those across America, were more concerned in the 1920s with zoning, as pioneered in Los Angeles, and with the details of altering transportation networks to meet the needs of the automobile than with creating a functionally unified city.[98] Virgil Bogue's conception of a comprehensive plan for Seattle eroded.

Nonetheless, the Bogue Plan left a lasting imprint upon Seattle. While never implemented in its entirety, the Bogue Plan had an impact upon the city's development. Numerous individual improvements, especially in parks, transportation facilities, and harbor facilities were made over the years. In fact, most of the park plans were ultimately implemented. Perhaps even more importantly, the Bogue Plan kept alive the concept of planning. When Seattleites considered planning anew after World War II, some looked back on the Bogue Plan favorably "as an instance of scanning the palm of an entire city and attempting to forecast its future existence."[99] In 1972 the head of the Seattle Department of Human Resources wondered in an article written for one of the city's leading newspapers, if "in an age o subdivisions and domed stadiums, can we look back on the Civic Idea and not yearn for that nobler vision?"[100]

5

Portland Adopts the Bennett Plan

▼

As was true in the other Pacific Coast cities, the tremendous growth that occurred in Portland deeply concerned the residents of that metropolis in the opening years of the twentieth century. In a letter to Portland's mayor in 1912, a leading member of the Portland Medical Society voiced a complaint heard with increasing frequency. "During the last five years," he observed, "there has been a great increase in the quantity of smoke overhanging the city."[1] Later in the same year the head of a local engineering company made another oft-heard complaint. He noted, "The City of Portland, due to its wonderful growth, is already finding the congestion of its streets a handicap to its increase."[2]

Like urbanites in other Pacific Coast cities, Portland's residents came to view city planning as a way to control the effects of growth.[3] Portlanders went farther than the residents of Seattle, San Francisco, Oakland, and Los Angeles, however, in adopting a city plan as a guide for the future evolution of their city. Business leaders were in the forefront of the campaign. In backing civic improvements and planning, they equated public advances with private progress. Merchants especially thought that planning would create an environment in which their firms could prosper. Like their counterparts elsewhere on the Pacific Coast, they viewed beauty as having a definite economic value. "The day has come when the artistic sense is a factor with men who have means to invest," an influential Portland newspaper editorialized in 1909. "The savage who sheltered himself in caves cared nothing for lines of beauty, but the latter day man of capital is not a savage," concluded the paper, "His tepee was good enough for the purposes of the aborigine, but not for the men with big bank accounts."[4]

The Origins of Planning:
Parks and Expositions

As it had in Oakland and Seattle, city planning began in Portland with efforts to establish a park and boulevard system. The Oregon state legislature set up a park board for Portland in 1900, and the board immediately called for the creation of "a park system embracing riverside, mountains and plains . . . connected by wide boulevards." Such a system, board members thought, would benefit Portland economically and socially. "The beautifying of the city as a whole, the increased healthfulness of the people, the higher values to all property, the opening of beautiful suburbs and the true expansion of the commonwealth itself are involved," they claimed. Civic pride was also at stake. A park system would, they thought, "go far to make this the most beautiful city in the world"— strong words, considering that just a generation before Portland had been a stump town hacked out of a forest wilderness.[5] Nonetheless, several years later Portland still possessed only 136 acres of parklands at ten dilapidated sites.[6]

Accomplishments began in 1903, when the park board invited John C. Olmsted of the Olmsted Brothers—who was visiting Seattle to design a new park system there—to come south and draw up a park plan for Portland as well. For a five-thousand-dollar fee, Olmsted readily accepted the invitation. Olmsted reported that Portland needed a "park-system" composed of "park squares, playgrounds, small or neighborhood parks, large or suburban parks, scenic reservations, boulevards, and parkways." Particularly important would be a series of waterfront parks along the Willamette River. West of the river there would be a parkway along the crest of the West Hills, while large parks would be developed in the rapidly growing region east of the river. A set of parkways would loop from Sellwood to Mount Tabor and the Columbia River and then back to the Willamette at the University of Portland.[7]

Portlanders would, Olmsted thought, benefit economically, socially, and morally from his proposed system. Property owners would reap monetary rewards from the "increased valuations" that would occur on "lands bordering upon various parks and parkways." Portland as a whole would be improved by the tendency of parks to "draw to the city wealth, the taxation of which may more than repay the city for the outlay." Moreover, parks were, he argued, "a power for educating the people to better things . . . they improve public taste." In short, parks could be "exceedingly important factors in developing the healthfulness, morality, intelligence, and business prosperity" of the residents of Portland.[8]

As in Seattle, little came immediately of Olmsted's ideas, for Portlanders found themselves drawn into the vortex of more pressing events. Instead, smaller local developments—school garden and playground movements—preceded unified park planning. The proponents of gardens and playgrounds strongly believed they could change the character of children by changing their environment. In 1906 Portland's superintendent of schools began encouraging children to plant school gardens, an action that won praise for instilling in the children "an interest in productive operations, habits of useful industry instead of mischievous idleness." Proponents claimed, "Every unfolding flower and maturing root in which the children are interested will help to make better men and women of them, and so will help to make the next generation better than this."[9]

Closely allied to the school garden program was a playground movement. Sponsored by the Portland Woman's Club, the YMCA, and the People's Institute, this campaign, which also began in 1906, had strong middle-class backing. Advocates viewed playgrounds as instrumental in improving the health and morals of children: "It is certain, had any of the plans laid out eight years ago materialized there would not be so many boys and girls in their teens on probation or pleading before the juvenile court."[10] Public playgrounds also won support as "the great equalizer" where children of all classes and races could play together and develop "common interests."[11] A private group, the People's Institute, received public funding to operate the playgrounds initially and reported in 1908 that "Americans, Syrians, Chinese, Japanese, Italians, Swedish, Irish, French, Indians, and English" were using them. It is unclear whether or not blacks were allowed in.[12] In Portland the playground drive was more than a middle-class movement. In 1911 the city's Socialist party passed a resolution calling for the "creation of sufficient parks and playgrounds for the use and pleasure of our people and children."[13] Enjoying broad-based support, the park board established eight playgrounds by 1912, and an estimated 300,000 children attended them during that year.[14]

From those scattered beginnings, park advocates turned to Olmsted's more comprehensive park and boulevard scheme. In December 1906, a group of business and civic leaders came together as the Initiative of One Hundred to work for a $1 million park bond issue to be voted on in the following year. According to a newspaper report, park proponents argued that by constructing a park system Portland had "the greatest opportunity to make itself famous with the least expense to itself. They were concerned that Portland might fall behind other cities "favorably known through their fine parks."[15]

John C. Ainsworth, one of Portland's leading businessmen, led the fight for the park bonds. Ainsworth had interests in banking, transportation, and manufacturing, and would be very active in the city planning campaign. Of well-established "old" wealth, Ainsworth would take a role in Portland's city improvement and planning movements over the coming decade roughly similar to those played by James Phelan in San Francisco and Frank Mott in Oakland. Like his business counterparts to the south, Ainsworth saw private business enterprises and public planning efforts as going together hand in hand. He viewed the political arena as a necessary place in which to work out ideas for the commercial advance of Portland. Like Phelan, Ainsworth harbored a sense of civic pride and patriotism. He once observed, "I think our trouble in the United States has been that we have judged success far too much by the money making yardstick." In fact, he concluded, "The leaders of art and literature and religion and humanity have occupied far more imposing places in the world's history than men whose only claim to distiction has been in wealth accumulation."[16]

Not all businessmen favored the bonds, however. Opposition came from the United East Side Clubs, prefiguring a later split in Portland's business community on the implementation of city planning measures. The rapidly expanding East Side lacked city services already in place in the well-established West Side (the Willamette River separated Portland into two parts). East Side businessmen and residents consequently urged that bonds for more immediate necessities—streets, bridges, water, and sewers—be given precedence over the park bonds. Despite East Side opposition, the park bonds, which needed only a simple majority, won approval by a vote of 6,666 to 4,359.[17]

During the next six years, the mayor and the park board (now headed by E. T. Mische, who had worked for Olmsted's firm) used the bond funds to expand Portland's park system. They developed new parks and laid out some boulevards to link them. Boulevards were especially important, one proponent claimed, because they would preserve "the natural beauties of one of the finest of the Western gateways of the city."[18] Nonetheless, opposition to the expansion of parks and boulevards surfaced. The widening of the boulevards displaced some residents, leading the Portland *Labor Press* to protest that "for a long time the industrious poor have been hit by this thing and robbed by that without being able to detect the holder of the bludgeon or catch the thief."[19] Such opposition had only a limited effect. More serious was a lack of funds, for the $1 million did not go far enough. Most of the money went into developing neighborhood parks. Although Portland possessed fifteen parks and thirteen playgrounds by 1913, the city had scarcely begun to put together the park system called for by Olmsted and still trailed Los Angeles, San Francisco, and Seattle in the number of parkland acres available on a per capita basis.[20]

If parks were one inspiration for planning in Portland, the Lewis and Clark Exposition of 1905 was a second. Although the immediate and direct impact of the exposition upon city planning was quite limited, its long-range impact, like that of the Alaska-Yukon-Pacific Exposition on Seattle four years later, was substantial. The park movement and the exposition jointly inspired Portland's planning advocates with a sense that they could control and alter their urban environment for the better.

The Lewis and Clark Exposition owed its existence to J. M. Long of the Portland Board of Trade, who organized a provisional committee in 1900 to discuss the staging of a Northwest Industrial Exposition. A bit later the Oregon Historical Society, led by the editor of the *Oregonian*, suggested the date and the theme. At the end of 1901, a private corporation, funded mainly by Portland's merchants and bankers, came into being to run the fair. A federal appropriation of $475,000 passed in 1904 provided additional funding, and the exposition was constructed on swampy ground around Guild's Lake near the Willamette River just to the northwest of Portland. The exposition opened on June 1, 1905, and by the time it closed its gates four and a half months later, 2.5 million people had visited it.[21]

As with Seattle's fair four years later, the main goals of those putting on the Lewis and Clark Exposition were to win national recognition for their city and to advertise the products of its businesses. One exposition advocate argued as early as 1901 that "a dominant desire connected with the proposed fair is that through it the Pacific Northwest shall be brought into larger and closer trade relations with the rest of the world, more particularly the nations of the Orient."[22] Another Portlander, who would become a proponent of city planning, later recalled that "the purpose of the Lewis and Clark Exposition in 1905 was to advertise the city and promote its growth." In fact, "the slogan shouted and printed at the time was 'Portland great, Portland fine! Five hundred thousand in Nineteen-nine!' "[23]

As would also be the case in Seattle, however, there was more to Portland's world's fair than economics, for the exposition exposed Portlanders to the idea of organized beauty. John C. Olmsted laid out the grounds for the Lewis and Clark Exposition. His formal design resembled that of Chicago's Columbian Exposition of 1893. A strong northerly axis was oriented to views of the Willamette River and Mount St. Helens. Whitewashed buildings of the Spanish Renaissance style were grouped between the river, Guild's Lake, and hills to the west, creating an impressive overall visual effect. Portland's mayor called it "a diamond set in a coronet of emeralds."[24]

The diamonds soon turned to dust. The physical structures

composing the exposition were only temporary. As early as 1903, members of the park board predicted that because the fair was constructed on land leased, not owned, by the city "most of the improvements will either disappear or revert to private use."[25] That prediction proved accurate. At the close of the fair, manufacturers developed the exposition site as an industrial district, and during the next few years even Guild's Lake was filled in and put to business use. Lacking the necessary funds, the city council passed up the possibility of turning the area into a park as desired by Olmsted. The apparent inability of Portlanders to capitalize on the fair has led the historian H. Kimbark MacColl to conclude that the Lewis and Clark Exposition was "a colossal missed chance."[26]

That assessment is only partly correct, for the exposition along with the park movement helped prepare the way for later city planning efforts. Both the exposition and the park work stressed the need for systematic, rather than piecemeal, approaches to the environment; and both combined beauty with economic gain. Utility and beauty, which would be the two dominant themes in Portland's city planning campaign, were present in those earlier movements.

The Bennett Plan

Sustained, organized efforts to improve Portland through planning began shortly after the closing of the exposition. In 1906 members of the Board of Trade, acting in consultation with Mayor Harry Lane, formed a Committee of One Hundred. Composed of representatives from each precinct of Portland, the committee consisted almost solely of business and professional men.[27] At its first meeting, Francis McKenna, a leading Portland real estate developer who had supported establishing the committee, stated that its goals were the municipal construction of a beltline railroad along Portland's waterfront on the Willamette River, the building of public docks, and the creation of a system of parks and boulevards throughout the city. Within a week, municipal ownership of coal gas and light plants had been added to the Committee of One Hundred's plans. They intended much more than beautification.

McKenna, who became the committee's president, explained, "The objects of the organization are to promote the moral, social, and financial welfare of Portland."[28]

Sometimes led by the Committee of One Hundred, but often working through smaller neighborhood associations, Portland residents labored to improve their city over the next four years. Civic pride underlay their moves. "Portland is an expanding city," observed the city's leading newspaper, the *Oregon Journal*. "It is no longer a provincial town." Improvements were needed because "the plant with which it has been operating is not big enough for the city that is to be." The journal, which Ainsworth controlled, concluded by comparing Portland to a business. "In private business, when the plant is outgrown it is added to, or discarded altogether, and a larger and more modern one is provided. The rule has to be applied to municipal life or the corporation can not enlarge."[29]

Civic improvements assumed several forms. Street widening and paving attracted attention from Portlanders who were worried lest their city "be left far in the rear of Pacific Coast progress," especially when compared with street improvements being undertaken in Seattle.[30] Neighborhood improvement clubs tried to restrict the erection of billboards and overhead street wires.[31] At the urgings of the clubs, the city constructed new bridges across the Willamette River to join the west and east sides of Portland.[32] Campaigns for better service from street railroad companies enlivened local politics. In 1909, for example, the Peninsula Development League, the United East Side Push Clubs, the Seventh Ward League, and the Holladay and Irvington Associations joined forces in a partially sucessful drive for improved streetcar service. Charles K. Henry, a real estate developer who headed the movement, explained its purpose: "What is the use of subscribing as I and others have done for country clubs, beautifying the city, livestock shows, etc., if we cannot get adequate car service?"[33]

At the same time, there was a growing perception that only city planning could solve Portland's problems. The *Oregon Journal* published editorial after editorial on the benefits of planning. The newspaper argued that Portlanders could win national recognition for their city through planning. An editorial asserted, "Portland has reached a size now that justifies it in moving out and up on broader and higher lines, the end in view being the most generally attractive city in the United States."[34] Noting that Portland could also best keep up with its urban rivals on the Pacific Coast through planning, the newspaper called for more paved streets, public docks, the construction of a civic center, and additional parks and boulevards. The newspaper also argued repeatedly that an improved city would instill Portlanders with higher moral values and lessen the incidence of crime. As one editorial explained: "The moral benefit more than pays for all the cost of city beautification. Crime and vice do not flourish amid broad avenues and open thoroughfares. . . . Crime cannot live among beautiful things, so every new civic building, every new statue, every additional foot of park or playground means a big gain for health and morality."[35]

New organizations—some ephemeral, others long-lived—arose to push the cause of civic improvement and planning. A Better Citizenship Association, a loose federation of religious leaders formed to "promote civic righteousness," came and went with little lasting impact upon Portland.[36] More important was the organization in 1909 of the Architectural League of the Pacific Coast. In its founding year a local branch of the league, the Portland Architectural Club, working in conjunction with the Portland Art Association, sponsored an exhibit "to stimulate a civic pride and an appreciation of things beautiful."[37] The club's president also called for the drafting of a plan for parks, boulevards, and public buildings. Local architects won praise for building several planned communities. Most notable was the construction of Mission Villa, a group of apartments for eight hundred people surrounded by parks and playgrounds. Made available to persons of moderate means, the complex won approval from the Portland *Labor Press* as a "fraternal village."[38]

From scattered movements, Portlanders went on to form the City Beautiful Committee in the fall of 1909. Oregon Senator Jonathan Bourne was particularly important in establishing the committee. Bourne had known Daniel Burnham when Burnham was working on his plan for Washington, D.C., and did his best to convince Portland's business leaders to set up the City Beautiful Committee as a means of implementing Burnham's concepts in their city. Attending the first meeting of the City Beautiful Committee were Portland's leading merchants, realtors, architects, publishers, and insurance men. Ainsworth, perhaps the most influential member of the committee, provided continuity with the earlier Committee of One Hundred. The City Beautiful Committee immediately started raising money to bring a planner to Portland to draw up a city plan.[39] However, securing the funds had to await further organizational changes. J. R. Wetherbee, the president of the Commercial Club and a member of Portland's park board, led the effort to establish a new body to campaign for city planning. Ainsworth and Charles Merrick, an insurance broker, assisted Wetherbee. All of those men had been active in earlier planning or improvement organizations. The new interim body, called a "city practical committee" by the Portland press, soon gave way to a more long-lasting organization.[40]

That organization was the Civic Improvement League. About one hundred prominent businessmen and professionals—described by the *Oregon Journal* as composing "the largest and most influential financial interests in Portland"—participated in the founding of the league on December 7, 1909. For permanent officers they chose men well versed in Portland's planning movement: Wetherbee as chairman, William Killingsworth (a Portland realtor) as vice-chairman, Merrick as secretary, and Ainsworth as treasurer. A fifteen-member executive committee drawn from the ranks of Portland's leading insurance men, architects, bankers, merchants, and lawyers would advise the league's officers and help carry on the day-to-day work. Like San Franciscans, who had formed the Association for the Improvement and Adornment of San Francisco to work for the Burnham Plan, Portlanders thus chose a private association to press for city planning.[41]

From the outset, league members stressed the practical benefits of planning. As one newspaper supporting the league observed, "the Civic League of Portland meditates no topsy-turvy upheaval in the city in order to construct the Greater Portland." The league, it continued, "simply designs to formulate a plan which may be followed by systematic and economic installing of improvements as the city grows. . . . People are not to pay more taxes as a result of planning, but less."[42] The need for harbor improvements, better streets, a civic center, and more parks was discussed at the founding of the league.

The Civic Improvement League quickly raised twenty thousand dollars to fund planning, with large contributions from Portland's major lumber, manufacturing, real estate, and banking companies. Ainsworth and Bourne gave generously and were very active in persuading others to contribute.[43] The league engaged Edward H. Bennett to prepare the plan for a fee of five hundred dollars per month. A 1902 graduate of the Ecole des Beaux-Arts, Bennett had assisted Burnham in drawing up city plans for San Francisco and Chicago. Thirty-five years old in 1909, this English architect was at the height of his powers. With the hiring of Bennett, the secretary of the league could report just one week after that body's founding that "we are getting along splendidly in our work."[44]

In contrast to the situation in most other Pacific Coast cities, the planning movement in Portland developed with less in the way of clear-cut ties to urban progressivism. Over the years, political fiqures of various persuasion backed the planning campaign and none came out publicly against it. Even Mayor Joseph Simon (1910–11), a standpat conservative who opposed city ownership of Portland's docks, backed the nascent city beautiful movement. A. G. Rushlight, who succeeded Simon as mayor, quickly became a tireless campaigner against vice and prostitution as well as a strong proponent of the municipal ownership of public utilities and docks. He also actively backed the adoption of the Bennett Plan in a manner reminiscent of Mayor Frank Mott's support for planning in Oakland. In short, city planning attracted political support of various hues in Portland.[45]

Given a free hand, Bennett worked on his plans for Portland throughout 1910. He labored mainly on his own, with the help of only a few assistants. The consideration of local ideas that characterized the preparation of Seattle's Bogue Plan was less evident in the drafting of a plan for Portland. As Merrick later observed, one of Bennett's more prominent characteristics was "his unwillingness to accept suggestions or direction." Bennett, he recalled, "gave all of us to understand that he had been employed to draw the plan and that he did not welcome any suggestion from any contributor."[46]

Bennett presented preliminary sketches to the Civic Improvement League in February 1911 and final ones at the end of the summer. The experiences of San Francisco with planning clearly influenced Bennett. Upon presenting his final sketches, he noted that San Franciscans were seriously considering the construction of a civic center in preparation for the Panama–Pacific International Exposition and concluded that "there can be no reason for doubting that the Portland plan will prove as valuable [as the Burnham Plan for San Francisco]."[47]

Like his mentor, Burnham, Edward Bennett thought in large terms. He planned for Portland's future as a city of two million people, a metropolis roughly ten times as populous as the Portland that existed in 1911. Like Burnham, Bennett believed that the different functions of a city should be segregated by area. Planning would further the separation and at the same time link the functions of the city in the interests of economic efficiency. "The ideal," Bennett wrote, "is the organic city with its parts and activities closely related and well defined, but not conflicting; wisely and economically builded, not a cluster of villages, each with its center, and with boundaries accidentally merged."[48]

Central to the Bennett Plan was the rebuilding of Portland's harbor on the Willamette River. As in the other Pacific Coast cities, the finishing of the Panama Canal acted as a spur to action, for Bennett thought that the "completion of the Panama Canal will bring a large marine business here." Bennett called for the deepening of the river channel, the public construction and ownership of new piers and warehouses, and the building of a beltline railroad to serve the waterfront—goals very similar to those held by the Committee of One Hundred as early as 1906. Bennett's belief in the need to segregate the different functions of Portland was most apparent in his treatment of waterways. The Bennett Plan encouraged the movement of shipping and manufacturing to the northwest, downstream from the established downtown district, thus freeing Portland's central waterfront for freight wagons and railroads supplying downtown wholesalers. Bennett argued that a modernized port would help Portland socially as well as economically, for, he claimed, his plan would eliminate saloons and brothels, which exerted "a subconscious influence upon citizenship [that] is extremely bad."[49]

To link Portland with its harbor and to improve communications within the city, Bennett envisioned major transportation changes. Like many other planners, he viewed streets as "arteries . . . for the life blood of the city, its traffic." Bennett called for the superimposition of radial traffic arteries stretching twenty miles to the southeast upon Portland's existing gridiron street plan and urged the construction of additional bridges and tunnels to

Edward Bennett envisioned uniform building heights and wide arterial streets for downtown Portland. From the Bennett Plan for Portland.

improve communications between Portland's east and west sides.[50] Noting that "the commercial supremacy of the City may in time be dependent upon a small fraction of a cent per ton for handling," Bennett also sought to improve railroad traffic into Portland. He concluded that "great railroad clearing and transfer yards" should be located on the Columbia Flats in touch with the docks designed for deep sea shipping."[51]

Bennett recommended a civic center consisting of a new courthouse, a city hall, a public library, and other buildings for the area around Portland's Lownsdale and Chapman squares. "The grouping of important public buildings," claimed Bennett, would be useful "both for convenience in the administration of municipal affairs and for nobility of purpose." Bennett also called for the building of a union railroad station to be linked by boulevards to the center of the city and the civic center, "thus producing a harmonious, highly efficient grouping of superb beauty," and the creation of a "recreation center" composed of a public auditorium, an academy, and a museum of fine arts near the Multnomah Club in downtown Portland.[52]

Finally, Bennett wanted major additions to Portland's system of parks and boulevards to "make of Portland preeminently the City Beautiful . . . encouraging the highest standard of citizenship." Bennett promoted the creation of both "great woodland or forest reserve areas" and "small neighborhood parks" needed for the "daily refreshment of the people." Bennett's concern about environmental influences upon people led him to consider combining parks with housing. Influenced by England's Garden City experiments, Bennett called for the opening of park-like suburbs for the working classes. "Modern transportation makes it possible to live in the outskirts, though work be in the center, and for each citizen to obtain thus a maximum of ground at a minimum cost," he noted. Workers, thought Bennett, "should always be provided with room for sunlight and air and charming surroundings. The cost is no greater. The efficiency of the citizenship of the people who live therein is vastly increased."[53]

Bennett viewed his plan for Portland as helping the city's residents economically. Above all, it would allow them to handle the rapid expansion of their city then occurring and to prepare for future growth. "No city of the Pacific Coast with hope for expansion beyond present limits has failed to provide itself with a plan,"

Edward Bennett's plan called for new parks to be established on the east and west sides of Portland. From the Bennett Plan for Portland.

Bennett explained. Planning would accomplish those goals at the lowest possible cost, for, Bennett asserted, "the cost will be measurably less than in haphazard growth."[54] Appealing to Portland's business leaders, Bennett compared a city to a business and claimed that planning benefited both. "The most successful businessman is he who has the most orderly and best directed 'plant,'" Bennett claimed. "The same principle may be applied to the city."[55]

While he stressed the economic aspects of planning, Bennett also valued highly the expected social benefits. A well-planned city with parks, boulevards, and a civic center would, he thought, inspire Portlanders with citizenship values and lessen friction between different groups in the city. Bennett predicted, "The greater City will result in higher citizenship" because "it militates alike against the selfish interest and the narrow view."[56]

The Campaign for the Bennett Plan

The first political test of Bennett's ideas came in the summer of 1911 as he was putting the final touches on his sketches for his plan. In June Portlanders voted on a $600,000 bond issue to build a public auditorium at an undecided site. The auditorium proposal won especially strong support from the Commercial Club, whose members were Portland's leading merchants and bankers, as a way of attracting conventions. Its business backers argued that the auditorium would further "Portland's development into a convention city of national possibilities."[57] Not all favored the bond issue, however. Some segments of organized labor opposed it, because they feared it would be built with nonunion labor and because it threatened to raise their taxes.[58] The bonds won approval by a vote of 13,915 to 10,771.[59]

From thats auspicious start, Portlanders advanced the cause of planning through the formation of yet another private association. In September 1911, the Civic Improvement League called a meeting of representatives from business organizations and neighborhood improvement clubs to set up a broadly based orga-

143

nization to secure public approval for the Bennett Plan. Some one hundred business and civic leaders attended the conference, including officers of the Chamber of Commerce and the Commerce Club, but no representatives of organized labor.[60] From that and other meetings emerged the Greater Portland Plans Association (GPPA) several months later.

As its founders had hoped, the GPPA was composed of a broad spectrum of Portland's business, professional, and political leaders—a body of considerable potential clout indeed. Merrick was chosen president, and John Haak (a lumberman), M. G. Munley, Dr. Andrew Smith, John Carroll (the editor of the *Evening Telegram*), Charles Morden (the assistant manager of the *Oregonian*), and Edmund Sawyer (an entrepreneur engaged in a variety of enterprises) won election as vice-presidents. Bankers, merchants, and lawyers composed the new organization's executive board (Wetherbee was a member). Many of those belonging to the GPPA, such as Ainsworth, had been members of earlier planning organizations in Portland; but the GPPA also included the city's mayor, park superintendent, and city engineer in its ranks.[61]

With their organization perfected, members of the GPPA turned to the question of how to win public approval for the adoption of the Bennett Plan. Like so many reformers in the Progressive Era, they placed their faith in the value of education. One GPPA leader observed, "It is only necessary to explain to any intelligent person the scope and intent of the plan to secure his or her heartiest support and commendation."[62] To that end, GPPA members sponsored numerous talks before local improvement clubs and held mass rallies complete with torchlight parades to publicize the Bennett Plan. The mayor declared February 29, 1912, to be Greater Portland Day. At 10:30 that morning, signaled by blasts of factory whistles, scores of GPPA canvassers spread out through the city to sign up new members and to win financial support for their organization. The GPPA persuaded the city government to publish twenty-five thousand copies of the plan and to distribute them to organizations of all types. Finally, in August 1912, the GPPA won inclusion for the Bennett Plan on the ballot for city elections to be held three months later.[63]

During the fall, the members of the GPPA redoubled their efforts. Boasting that their organization had more than four thousand members, they sent out letters to all of Portland's business groups asking for public declarations of their support. The results were gratifying. At a mass meeting in late October, every major business group came out in support of the plan, including the Commercial Club, Chamber of Commerce, Rotary Club, the Ad Club, the Transportation Club, and the Progressive Merchants' Association. Businessmen were particularly susceptible to the economic arguments made by their colleagues in the GPPA, for, like Bennett, members of the GPPA stressed the monetary benefits they expected to result from planning. They argued that only through systematic planning could Portland prepare for the increases in commerce and immigration expected to come from the opening of the Panama Canal and thus stay abreast of its urban rivals, Seattle and San Francisco. Nor, they claimed, would planning prove expensive. To the contrary, by avoiding costly blunders as Portland grew, GPPA members asserted that planning would lower their city's tax rates, thus creating an attractive business environment likely to draw new industry to Portland. Planning champions claimed, "The plan involves no extraordinary expenditures, but simply seeks to adapt the units of improvement to a coherent plan as the city grows."[64]

Running through the arguments of the members of the GPPA and the businessmen supporting them was a belief that their city was destined for greatness. A desire for acceptance of Portland as a regional leader and as a national city of some substance motivated planning proponents in Portland, just as it did those in Seattle. A poem published by the GPPA caught well these wishes:

Wake up a bit, my Portland friend,
And as you boost for farm and tillage,
Don't overlook the fact meanwhile
That Portland's not a brushwood village.

And great as Portland is today,
It's just as well to figger
That she will keep on year by year,
Still getting bigger, bigger, bigger.

When she is in the million class,
Say, fellow, wouldn't it be bitter

145

If we had left her streets and squares
So doggone small they wouldn't fit her?

Then hit the highway to the polls
And fix our city's weal forever.
Endorse the Bennett Plans and be
A first class little boosting lever.[65]

No organized resistance to the adoption of the Bennett Plan surfaced. The Portland Central Labor Council, which claimed eight thousand members, remained neutral on the issue. After listening to the president of the GPPA discuss the Bennett Plan in early February 1912, Central Labor Council members expressed their general approval of it. Two months later they passed a resolution calling for the construction of a proposed city library "in accord with the plans promulgated by the Greater Portland Plans Association." They also agreed, however, with the Oregon State Grange that good county roads were more important than "highways and boulevards . . . in order that a few pleasure seekers may enjoy themselves." In the end they decided that the Bennett Plan was "of no importance whatever at this time" and recommended neither a favorable nor a negative vote on it.[66]

The Bennett Plan won approval at the polls by the overwhelming majority of 16,202 to 7,996.[67] The ballot issue called upon the city council to follow the Bennett Plan in "making public improvements of any kind . . . *as far as in their judgment is practicable and advantageous*" [italics added]. With the economy of their city booming, all groups could agree that planning was needed for Portland to take full advantage of the opportunities for expansion. The splits among different business groups and between business organizations and other groups that had hindered the adoption of city plans in San Francisco and Seattle did not surface in Portland in 1912. The qualifying phrase "as far as in their judgment is practicable and advantageous" made the Bennett Plan seem more flexible than many other city plans. It was the lack of such flexibility that, in part, killed Seattle's Bogue Plan that same year.

The Erosion of the Bennett Plan

Whether the Bennett Plan could be implemented remained to be seen, however. The very flexibility of the plan raised questions for the future. In fact, signs in the 1912 election hinted that disagreements would soon make putting it into practice difficult.

A $2 million park bond issue closely associated with the Bennett Plan went down to defeat in 1912. Business leaders, including the heads of the Commercial Club and the Chamber of Commerce, argued for the park bonds because parks were likely to attract visitors and settlers to Portland. Lecturers for Portland's newly created Social Service Council also pointed out that, as alternatives to saloons and pool halls, playgrounds would improve the morals of young people.[68] However, many Portlanders viewed the expansion of their city's park system as an unnecessary expense. Claiming that the park bonds would become a "mother of real estate graft" and that "the workingman has to pay all taxes directly or indirectly and will have to pay for this," the Central Labor Council urged their defeat.[69] The final tally was 9,346 favorable to 15,406 negative votes.[70]

The simultaneous approval of the Bennett Plan and the defeat of the park bonds should have given planning advocates pause. The Bennett Plan passed because Portlanders viewed it as a general guide that would aid the private business development of their city. The park bonds lost, for they were seen as a specific issue that would cost, not save, money. However, difficulties seemed far away to planning proponents in 1912. Elated by their victory in winning approval for the Bennett Plan, they expected nothing but continued successes in the future.

The strong organization forged by the GPPA continued to operate after the 1912 election. In 1913 the GPPA began publishing its own journal, *Greater Portland*, to promote the cause of planning. More than in the past, GPPA members stressed the moral and social benefits that they saw in planning. One planning advocate wrote, "There is nothing that will so elevate citizenship, promote civic pride and self respect as to act together in adopting units of the city's inevitable growth to a systematic plan."[71] Parks and playgrounds were seen as especially useful. The lack of enough mod-

147

ern playgrounds was, in the minds of advocates of a planned city, "linked to juvenile delinquency and inefficiency in school." Moreover, it was expected that the problem would worsen as immigrants of very diverse backgrounds thronged to Portland with the opening of the Panama Canal. "If Portland is going to handle the tremendous physical, moral, and social problems incident to the coming of a large number of immigrants it will have to do better," noted one GPPA member.[72] Portlanders welcomed continuing growth for their city, but only if they could control its social and economic consequences.

While placing a new emphasis on the social advantages of planning, GPPA members continued to claim economic benefits. The newly elected president of the GPPA, who was the head of the Sherman Clay Company, summarized what many believed. "In the building of a great city it is essential that we have a plan," he asserted, "that we have broad arteries for trade, that we have adequate and suitable docks, that we improve our harbor, that we develop our terminal yards so our shipping may be carried on properly." He concluded, "We should get away from the idea some have put forth that the Bennett Plan is for a city beautiful, and commence to talk in a sane and practical way about a city practical—the Bennett Practical Plan."[73]

Despite the continued work of the GPPA, the implementation of the Bennett Plan never occurred. The concept of comprehensive city planning began eroding less than a year after the 1912 election, as foretold by the failure of the park bond issue. While Portlanders could—like Seattleites—agree that having a planned city was valuable in the abstract, they were no more successful than other Pacific Coast urbanites in putting their plans into practice. They soon divided on the specific proposals in the Bennett Plan. The GPPA did succeed in having a city planning commission set up in July 1913 to advise the city council on the implementation of the Bennett Plan. The commission succeeded in having the federal government construct a new post office in conformance with the Bennett Plan, but it met defeat on other major issues. The commission failed to win locations prescribed in the plan for the building of an art gallery and a civic auditorium, failed to secure approval for new street plans, and incurred defeat on park issues.

The difficulty in locating the civic auditorium, the bonds for which had been approved by voters two years before, proved most damaging. Like the siting of the civic center in Seattle, choosing the location for the auditorium in Portland split businessmen into warring camps. East Side and West Side businessmen argued for the siting of the auditorium on their sides of the Willamette River. After a protracted and bitter dispute, they agreed on a compromise site unrelated to the Bennett Plan.[74] Nearly as serious was the defeat of the plan's proposal to widen Burnside Street, an avenue Bennett had designated to become one of Portland's major traffic arteries. Property owners along Burnside Street, working through their own local improvement organization, opposed the efforts of the GPPA to alter Burnside, for they feared that any changes might decrease their property values.[75]

Capping those disappointments was the failure to win approval for $2 million in park bonds in a renewed campaign in the fall of 1913. Park advocates put foward the familiar arguments in favor of the bonds. Chamber of Commerce officers emphasized that the bonds would be a "good investment for the city" by bringing people to Portland.[76] With the completion of the Panama Canal fast approaching, proponents stressed that parks would help integrate the expected massive influx of immigrants with the rest of the city's population. In a letter sent to all of Portland's ministers, the superintendent of parks claimed that the passage of the park bonds "will be one of the most favorable steps ever taken in the City of Portland toward the solution of many of our social problems and toward the prevention of social evils that must necessarily threaten the city upon the opening of the Panama Canal."[77] Nonetheless, the bonds were again defeated, this time by the resounding vote of 15,781 to 23,402.[78] While no organized opposition to the bonds existed, most Portlanders probably reasoned that other projects were more urgent than park and boulevard extensions.

With those setbacks, the planning commission established by the GPPA in 1913 ceased to function just one year later, and city planning advocates in Portland, paralleling what was then taking place in Seattle, turned to more limited projects. Portland's schools sponsored an "earth education" movement that gave prizes to the best school gardens.[79] City officials joined with neighborhood improvement clubs in drives to clean up vacant lots and to eliminate public nuisances.[80] Like their counterparts in Pacific Coast cities to the north and the south, Portland's realtors also worked with streetcar companies in the years just before World War I to develop middle-class suburbs around the fringes of their city.[81]

By 1914 the implementation of the Bennett Plan was at a standstill. The outbreak of war disrupted the economy of the Pacific Northwest and plunged Portland into a recession, distracting Portlanders from city planning.[82] Even before the war, however, divisions separating different groups had greatly limited the ability of Portlanders to put the Bennett Plan into practice.

Looking back over his work for the Bennett Plan in 1945, one former planning advocate lamented that Portland derived "little more" from the plan "than some beautiful illustrations, now almost forgotten."[83] That judgment was too harse. If Portlanders proved incapable of implementing all aspects of the Bennett Plan, they did benefit from the adoption of parts of it and from civic improvements made independently of the plan. Many of the parks, street and transportation improvements, harbor facilities, and civic buildings first suggested by Bennett won approval over the years. As in Seattle, individual accomplishments typified the legacy of Progressive-Era city planning in Portland.

6

Patterns and Stages in
City Planning

▼

The study of city planning on the Pacific Coast contributes to our understanding of American history in three ways. Most importantly, it refines our knowledge of the Progressive Era, and especially the politics involved in city planning during that period. It also extends our understanding of the development of western cities at the close of their frontier periods of growth. Finally, it enhances our knowledge of the ways by which businessmen have tried to shape their social, political, and economic environments in the United States.

Progressive-Era City Planning

Many historians have concluded that an appropriate way to view the Progressive Era is to see that period as one in which Americans were reordering their lives in the wake of disruptions

caused by rapid industrialization and urbanization. The city planning movements on the Pacific Coast represented efforts to take
advantage of opportunities and handle problems resulting from
the economic transformation that was occurring in that region as
elsewhere in the United States. A major theme was the replacement of a personal, face-to-face society by a more highly organized,
bureaucratic society. Businesses run by management hierarchies,
nationwide labor unions, farm cooperatives, and professional
organizations spread across the land. Professional expertise came
to count for more than personal connections in American life, and
informal ways of doing things gave way to working through formal,
bureaucratic organizations.

The businessmen who were so important to Pacific Coast city
planning partook of the growing organization of American life,
and the organizational synthesis approach to modern American
history helps explain their actions. Even such well-known business leaders as James Phelan of San Francisco and John Ainsworth
of Portland found it essential to work through organizations to
achieve their goals. Chambers of commerce, commercial clubs,
boards of trade, and other business organizations were very important in supporting planning. Local improvement clubs, which
drew much of their strength from neighborhood businessmen,
proliferated in all of the cities. Citywide organizations soon followed. Businessmen set up some, such as the Association for the
Improvement and Adornment of San Francisco, as a way to work
around the established political system, which they viewed as unresponsive to their wishes. Others, such as the Greater Portland
Plans Association, worked within the established political system.
Those opposed to planning, such as the south-end businessmen in
Seattle, also worked through organizations. Nor were businessmen alone. Professionals—especially architects, engineers, and
lawyers—formed their own organizations, such as local chapters
of the American Institute of Architects, to work in coalition with
the business groups.

With its stress on the growing desire for order and efficiency,
the organizational synthesis approach to history explains well the
thoughts and attitudes of the businessmen in the forefront of the
planning campaigns on the Pacific Coast. Confronted with the
burgeoning growth of their cities, businessmen viewed planning
as a key method to channel the forces of change. They argued that

only city planning could ensure the orderly and efficient development of their cities. Only through planning by experts, they believed, could the construction of new harbor facilities, street and transportation systems, and civic centers be properly coordinated so that their cities would function as harmonious entities rather than as discordant collections of separate parts. Further, businessmen anticipated that such integrated developments would save tax dollars spent on public services while simultaneously boosting private profits by providing facilities that would encourage the development of trade and manufacturing.

Such developments would, business leaders thought, help put their cities on the map as part of America's urban network and aid them greatly in their rivalries with other Pacific Coast cities. They were proud of their cities and sought, through planning, recognition for them as the equals of cities in other, longer settled sections of the country. They hoped such recognition would serve them well in their continued quest for growth. People, capital, and businesses would all, they anticipated, gravitate to attractive, well-designed centers. At the same time, they were conscious of the ties their cities maintained with their regional hinterlands and were always concerned about the actions of their neighbors. Intercity rivalry motivated many of those engaged in planning. Only through the adoption of well-modeled plans, they argued, could their cities either catch up with or move ahead of other cities on the Pacific Coast.

A desire to maintain their influence over new groups entering their cities also led businessmen to spearhead planning movements. Businessmen saw parks, municipal ornaments, and civic centers as tools by which they might harmonize the often clashing values of the many different groups in their cities. Through planning they hoped to unite neighborhoods separated by ethnic, economic, and geographic barriers. Planning came to mean building functional cities whose residents were bound together by a sense of civic unity and civic patriotism.

In their leadership and support of the planning campaigns, businessmen blurred the boundaries separating public from private actions. They saw no sharp separation between what they were doing to build up their business enterprises as private citizens and what they could accomplish through politics. Public planning was for most of them an extension of their private work.

Thus, for example, Frank Mott became deeply involved in real estate development even as he sponsored city planning as Oakland's mayor.

The city planning movements were often associated with progressivism.[1] Business leaders like Phelan in San Francisco were often active in the progressive campaigns of their cities, and many of the same business groups that backed planning (such as the Municipal League in Seattle) were also deeply involved in progressive reforms. That situation was hardly surprising. City planning proponents shared many assumptions and goals with Progressive-Era reformers. Most fundamentally, reformers and planners believed that people could be changed—and changed for the better—by altering their environments. People, they thought, could determine their own futures, could progress to new levels of development. Businessmen in the city planning movements believed that parks, boulevards, and civic centers would inspire all citizens with a vaguely defined sense of order and morality.

As illustrated in the works of the historian William Wilson and other scholars, the early city planning movement was much more than an aesthetic attempt to beautify cities. In his study of the city beautiful movement in five cities across the nation, Wilson concluded that "for all its idealistic rhetoric the movement was imbued with the courage of practicality, for it undertook the most difficult task of all, to accept human material where found, to take the city as it was and to refashion it into something better."[2] On the Pacific Coast, as well, businessmen favored planning because it sought to come to grips with what they saw as urban problems and opportunities. Nonetheless, the plans were inadequate for the tasks at hand. While viewed as comprehensive by people in the Progressive Era, the plans did not in reality deal with all urban problems. The planning focused more on the needs of the cities than on the needs of all of the people in them. They touched only lightly on housing, for instance. Only the Bogue Plan addressed anything approaching the full range of urban problems.

City planning on the Pacific Coast originated in diverse sources and passed through several definite stages. Planning often began with the efforts of business groups—especially merchants or real estate men—to improve certain sections of their cities, often the downtown districts. Street lighting and cleaning frequently headed the list of early civic improvements. Municipal decorations, street tree plantings, and water fountains were often included in the first stage of development.

From scattered local actions, planning proponents began thinking in terms of citywide improvements, a second stage in planning. The creation of park and boulevard systems was often the initial attempt to deal with city problems at more than the neighborhood level. The establishment of park systems, rather than simply individual parks, introduced people to the idea that they could shape their urban environments. In the park movements, too, urbanites were first exposed to the idea that beauty could have economic utility, a major theme put forward by the businessmen involved in the planning movement. Expositions—the Lewis and Clark Exposition, the Alaska-Yukon-Pacific Exposition, and the Panama–Pacific International Exposition—also spurred the development of planning. Like the world's fair in Chicago in 1893, the expositions awakened city dwellers to the possibilities of coordinated building.

From those efforts Pacific Coast businessmen moved on to a third stage in planning, the preparation of what they saw as comprehensive plans for their cities. It was this development that most clearly separated the city beautiful movements from earlier efforts at civic improvement. Sometimes working on their own, sometimes in conjunction with city officials, business-dominated organizations hired planners to come to their cities and draft guides for their future growth.

Variety characterized the resulting plans. Charles Robinson's plans for Oakland and Los Angeles dealt mainly with parks and boulevards, while Virgil Bogue's plan for Seattle emphasized new designs for that city's streets, transportation system, and harbor. In general, those plans prepared after 1909—a major transition point in planning history, when the city beautiful movement gave way to a city functional movement—were more highly engineered than the earlier plans. The plans for Portland and especially for Seattle dealt more with the details of harbors and streets than with parks and boulevards. Too much, however, should not be made of that division. All of the plans addressed the same major items and possessed the same basic goals. The differences among the plans were differences of degree, not kind.

The political contests over the acceptance of the plans composed the fourth stage. Business groups achieved only partial success in their efforts to secure public acceptance and adherence to the plans. The degrees to which they succeeded in winning approval for the plans depended on several factors. Those plans with limited goals were more likely to be implemented than those that sought to remake the cities in major ways. Robinson's plan for Oakland won greater acceptance than Burnham's plan for San Francisco. Those plans put forward as suggested, rather than mandatory, guides for the development of cities were more likely to be approved. Bogue's rigid plan for Seattle went down to defeat at the polls, while Bennett's flexible plan for Portland secured public acceptance. Political support could prove crucial in winning approval for planning. Mayor Frank Mott's strong backing of the Robinson Plan for Oakland helped obtain implementation for much of the plan.

The pattern of stages in the development of city planning in Pacific Coast cities, while discernable, was far from tidy. Different stages overlapped each other or were entirely absent in some cities. For instance, the park and boulevard movement, which was so important in all of the other Pacific Coast cities, was of only limited significance in San Francisco. Each city possessed its own pattern of development, making the planning movement complex.

Western City Planning

The distinctive features of each city also make it hard to generalize about the development of Seattle, Portland, Oakland, San Francisco, and Los Angeles as western cities; but some observations are possible through an examination of their planning movements. Despite their origins as "instant cities," the Pacific Coast metropolises were coming to resemble their eastern and midwestern counterparts by 1900 and 1910. The historian Lawrence Larson has argued that as early as the 1880s the towns of the trans-Mississippi West faced many of the same problems, and derived many of the same solutions, as eastern towns and cities. Larson has shown that as they matured, western centers came increasingly to resemble other cities in their architecture and cultural character.

In most respects the planning movements that occurred in the Pacific Coast cities were similar to those going on elsewhere in the United States in the same time period. The same basic stages and patterns of development can be found in the cities that Wilson has studied.[3] Well-established eastern planners, a tightly knit group of professionals who knew each other closely, prepared the plans for the western cities: John Olmsted, Daniel Burnham, Charles Robinson, Edward Bennett, and Virgil Bogue. Only Bogue had any particular knowledge of western cities, and even Bogue had to accept Olmsted as a partner. Not surprisingly, the plans drafted for the Pacific Coast cities differed little from those drawn up for cities elsewhere in America. The eastern planners were interested in turning Pacific Coast cities into "ideal" cities. Blindered by their previous training and work, they could do only what they had learned from their earlier experiences. Most made little effort to adjust their plans to take advantage of—or even acknowledge the existence of—the western environment. San Francisco and Portland would, in their visions, have become Washington, D.C., Chicago, or Paris. In the hilly Pacific Coast cities, for example, arterials and circumferentials would ride roughshod over the topography. In Seattle, even the native evergreen trees were to be replaced with deciduous trees from the East.

In its association with progressivism, city planning on the Pacific Coast also resembled planning in other regions of the United States. As Wilson and other scholars have demonstrated, planning and progressivism often went hand in hand in eastern and midwestern cities. In cities as diverse as New York, Chicago, Harrisburg, and Kansas City, city planning was associated with some aspects of urban progressivism. (Such an association was not, however, ubiquitous. Robert W. Speer, the city boss of Denver, was the single most important person in his city's planning movement.) In that respect, as in many others, city planning on the Pacific Coast was far from unique. Planning advocates there shared many of the same motivations of those operating elsewhere in America. The search for social harmony in their cities and the quest for recognition of their cities as urban centers of regional importance and national repute ran through the thoughts of many engaged in America's planning movement.[4]

However, a major event distinguished Pacific Coast planners from their national colleagues and motivated them. The tremendous importance of the coming completion of the Panama Canal in leading businessmen, especially merchants, into planning movements was a unique element on the Pacific Coast. The eagerness of business leaders in cities up and down the coast to prepare for the opening of the canal and their fears that their counterparts in rival cities would use the canal to get ahead of them lent an urgency to the involvement of businessmen in the planning campaigns not found everywhere in America.[5]

Progressive-Era Businessmen

Businessmen sought to shape their social and cultural environments in a number of ways during the Progressive Era. They reasserted control over their individual factories through scientific management, or Taylorism, and created new management structures. So, too, they tried to develop city planning as a tool with which to control the vagaries of their urban environments.

That businessmen were active in city planning should not come as a surprise. Although Americans have conventionally viewed businessmen as opponents of planning, historians have recently shown that some businessmen have worked for certain types of planning throughout the twentieth century. In fact, recent scholarship suggests that business involvement in planning has been pervasive.[6] Businessmen often turned to politics for the sometimes contradictory goals of trying to stabilize their competitive business environments, of seeking to win competitive advantages over each other, and of attempting to smooth out the ups and downs of the business cycle.[7] The roles businessmen played in city planning should, thus, be most properly viewed as part of a larger picture: the efforts of businessmen to use planning to seek advancement for their firms.

Businessmen wanted to encourage the social and economic growth of their cities. They were boosters. The thought of uncontrolled growth, however, disturbed many of them; and they hoped through planning to channel growth along paths that they desired. Growth with harmony was one of their primary goals. They wanted to replicate in their cities what they saw as the harmonious functioning of the many different parts of the pieces of machinery in their factories. Predictability and stability were their goals.

The limited success of businessmen in shaping their urban environments on the Pacific Coast is worth stressing in conclusion. In his examination of the city beautiful movement, Wilson concludes that planning accomplished a great deal. In addition to "tree-shaded boulevards, undulating parks, and graceful neoclassical buildings rich in ornament," the city beautiful movement "left a legacy of civic activism" and brought the professional planning expert to the fore.[8] All true, both on the Pacific Coast and nationally. As commercial cities, those on the Pacific Coast, like those studied by Wilson, possessed large middle classes of businessmen and professionals eager for planning. Moreover, in contrast to industrial cities in which planning was less successful, they did not have "a higher proportion of laborers likely to be skeptical of sweeping improvement plans."[9] It is important, however, to remember that in their major goal—the implementation of what they saw as comprehensive city plans—businessmen failed. The Pacific Coast cities contained too many different groups with different values for agreements to be reached on most aspects of city planning.

Planning was defeated in the political arena. All of the groups involved could agree that city planning in the abstract was valuable, but they reached few agreements on the concrete details. Various groups of businessmen fought each other. No monolithic business community existed in any of the Pacific Coast cities. In Seattle the issue of where to site the civic center split the business community. In Portland East Side and West Side business groups fought over how best to develop their city. In San Francisco the basic issue of how fast and by what means to rebuild after the earthquake and fire proved divisive. Moreover, divisions between business organizations and other groups killed the planning prospects. Labor organizations often opposed what business groups wanted. That type of division was most apparent in San Francisco, but it was significant in other cities as well, particularly Portland and Seattle. In the end, the city plans, which looked so beautiful to their proponents on paper, won only partial acceptance.

NOTES

INTRODUCTION

1. My findings reinforce those of William Issel in "'Citizens Outside of Government': Business and Public Policy in San Francisco and Los Angeles, 1890–1930," *Pacific Historical Review* 58 (May 1988): 117–46. In examining the roles businessmen played in the formation of urban policies, Issel concludes that "never a monolithic political bloc, business developed its political role in the urban policy-making process by a combination of bargaining and conflict with its rivals, and by accommodating to its internal differences, rather than by imposing its preferences upon the body politic . . . Divisions among businessmen and their need to work in ways that required cooperation and compromise did not stand in the way of political success; no other community interest groups rivaled business in its ability to influence the shaping of urban policy-making decisions in San Francisco and Los Angeles" (119–20).
2. Scholars have debated the degree to which American politics have been pluralistic or elitist for at least a generation. For classic works on the topic see Peter Bachrach and Morton Baratz, "Two Faces of Power," *American Political Science Review* 56 (December 1962):

947–52; Robert Dahl, *Who Governs?* (New Haven: Yale University Press, 1961); and Nelson Polsby, *Community Power and Political Theory* (New Haven: Yale University Press, 1963).

3. For a study stressing the importance of real estate interests in setting the parameters of city planning, see Marc A. Weiss, *The Rise of the Community Builders: The American Real Estate Industry and Urban Land Planning* (New York: Columbia University Press, 1987).

4. An extensive literature on businessmen and planning exists. See Guy Alchon, *The Invisible Hand of Planning: Capitalism, Social Science, and the State in the 1920s* (Princeton, New Jersey: Princeton University Press, 1985); Robert M. Collins, *The Business Response to Keynes, 1929–1964* (New York: Columbia University Press, 1981); Louis Galambos and Joseph Pratt, *The Rise of the Corporate Commonwealth: United States Business and Public Policy in the 20th Century* (New York: Basic Books, 1988); and Ellis W. Hawley, *The New Deal and the Problem of Monopoly* (Princeton: Princeton University Press, 1966).

5. *Vote for Progress,* pamphlet, Oakland, 1892, unpaged.

6. *Merchants Association Review,* October 1909.

7. Samuel P. Hays, *The Response to Industrialism, 1885–1914* (Chicago: University of Chicago Press, 1957); Robert Wiebe, *The Search for Order* (New York: Hill and Wang, 1967).

8. Louis Galambos, "The Emerging Organizational Synthesis in Modern American History," *Business History Review* 44 (Autumn 1970): 279–90; Galambos, "Technology, Political Economy, and Professionalization: Central Themes of the Organizational Synthesis," *Business History Review* 57 (Winter 1983): 471–93.

9. Alan Brinkley, "Writing the History of Contemporary America: Dilemmas and Challenges," *Daedalus* 113 (Summer 1984), 134.

10. John W. Reps, *The Making of Urban America: A History of City Planning in the United States* (Princeton: Princeton University Press, 1965); and Mellior Scott, *American City Planning Since 1890* (Berkeley: University of California Press, 1969).

11. Michael McCarthy, "Chicago Businessmen and the Burnham Plan," *Journal of the Illinois State Historical Society* 62 (Autumn 1970): 228–56; Jon Peterson, "The City Beautiful Movement: Forgotten Origins and Lost Meanings," *Journal of Urban History* 2 (August 1976): 415–34; Stanley Schultz and Clay McShane, "To Engineer the Metropolis: Sewers, Sanitation, and City Planning in Late-Nineteenth-Century America," *Journal of American History* 65 (September 1978): 389–411; and William Wilson, *The City Beautiful Movement in Kansas City* (Columbia: University of Missouri Press, 1964).

12. Wilson, "The ideology, aesthetics and politics of the City Beautiful

movement," in Anthony Sutcliffe, ed., *The Rise of Modern Urban Planning, 1800–1914* (New York: St. Martin's Press, 1980).

13. Christine Boyer, *Dreaming the Rational City: The Myth of American City Planning* (Cambridge: MIT Press, 1983).

14. Richard Fogelsong, *Planning the Capitalist City: The Colonial Era to the 1920s* (Princeton: Princeton University Press, 1986), 20, 23.

15. *Ibid.*, 125.

16. Christine Rosen, *The Limits of Power: Great Fires and the Process of City Growth in America* (Cambridge: Cambridge University Press, 1986).

17. Schultz, *Constructing Urban Culture: American Cities and City Planning, 1800–1920* (Philadelphia: Temple University Press, 1989), xvii, 184, and 213.

18. Wilson, *The City Beautiful* (Baltimore: Johns Hopkins University Press, 1989), 1.

19. *Ibid*, 2.

20. Gunther Barth, "Urbanization in the American West—A Review Article," *Business History Review* 58 (Summer 1984): 263–67; Oliver Knight, "Toward an Understanding of the Western Town," *Western Historical Quarterly* 4 (January 1973): 27–42; Lawrence Larsen and Robert Branyan, "The Development of an Urban Civilization on the Frontier of the American West," *Societas* 1 (Winter 1971): 33–50; Bradford Luckingham, "The City in the Westward Movement—A Bibliographic Note," *Western Historical Quarterly* 5 (July 1974): 295–306; Gilbert Stelter, "The City and Westward Expansion: A Western Case Study," *Western Historical Quarterly* 4 (April 1973): 187–202.

21. Carl Abbott, *Portland: Planning, Politics, and Growth in a Twentieth-Century City* (Lincoln: University of Nebraska Press, 1983); Beth Bagwell, *Oakland: The Story of a City* (Novato: Presidio Press, 1982); Robert M. Fogelson, *The Fragmented Metropolis: Los Angeles, 1850–1930* (Cambridge: Harvard University Press, 1967); Neal Hines, *Denny's Knoll: A History of the Metropolitan Tract of the University of Washington* (Seattle: University of Washington Press, 1980); William Issel and Robert Cherny, *San Francisco, 1865–1932: Politics, Power, and Urban Development* (Berkeley: University of California Press, 1986); Judd Kahn, *Imperial San Francisco: Politics and Planning in an American City, 1897–1906* (Lincoln: University of Nebraska Press, 1979); Roger Lotchin, *San Francisco, 1846–1856: From Hamlet to City* (New York: Oxford University Press, 1974); E. Kimbark MacColl, *The Growth of a City: Power and Politics in Portland, Oregon, 1915 to 1950* (Portland: Georgian Press, 1979); MacColl, *The Shaping of a City: Business and Politics in Portland, Oregon 1885 to 1915* (Portland: Georgian Press, 1976); Norbert Mac-Donald, *Distant Neighbors: A Comparative History of Seattle and*

Vancouver (Lincoln: University of Nebraska Press, 1987); and Roger Sale, *Seattle: Past to Present* (Seattle: University of Washington Press, 1976).

22. Duncan Aikman, ed., *The Taming of the Frontier* (New York: Minton, Balch and Company, 1925); Earl Pomeroy, *The Pacific Slope* (Seattle: University of Washington Press, 1965).

23. Barth, *Instant Cities: Urbanization and the Rise of San Francisco and Denver* (New York: Oxford University Press, 1975); Larsen, *The Urban West at the End of the Frontier* (Lawrence: Regents Press of Kansas, 1978); Gerald Nash, *The American West in the Twentieth Century: A Short History of an Urban Oasis* (Englewood Cliffs: Prentice-Hall, 1973); John Reps, *Cities of the American West: A History of Frontier Urban Planning* (Princeton: Princeton University Press, 1979).

24. Barth, *Instant Cities*, xxi.

25. Larson, *Urban West*, 120.

26. Thomas Cochran, *Business in American Life: A History* (New York: McGraw-Hill, 1972).

27. Alfred D. Chandler, Jr., *The Visible Hand: The Managerial Revolution in American Business* (Cambridge: Harvard University Press, 1977).

28. See: Burton W. Folsom, Jr., *Urban Capitalists: Entrepreneurs and City Growth in Pennsylvania's Lackawanna and Lehigh Regions, 1800–1920* (Baltimore: Johns Hopkins University Press, 1981).

CHAPTER 1

1. John S. Hittell, *A History of the City of San Francisco and Incidentally of the State of California* (San Francisco: A. L. Bancroft & Company, 1878), 6, 10.

2. Gerald Nash, *The American West in the Twentieth Century: A Short History of an Urban Oasis* (Englewood Cliffs: Prentice-Hall, 1973), ch. 1.

3. Robert Wiebe, *The Search for Order, 1877–1920* (New York: Hill and Wang, 1967).

4. Earl Pomeroy, *The Pacific Slope* (Seattle: University of Washington Press, 1965), ch. 6.

5. Gunther Barth, *Instant Cities: Urbanization and the Rise of San Francisco and Denver* (New York: Oxford University Press).

6. U. S. Bureau of the Census,.*Thirteenth Census of the United States, 1910, Abstract of the Census with a Supplement for California* (Washington, D.C., 1910), 63–65.

7. Roger W. Lotchin, *San Francisco, 1846–1856: From Hamlet to City* (New York: Oxford University Press, 1974), ch. 3.

8. William Issel and Robert Cherny, *San Francisco, 1865–1932: Politics, Power, and Urban Development* (Berkeley: University of California Press, 1986), ch. 2.

9. David Lavender, *Nothing Seemed Impossible: William Ralston and Early San Francisco* (Palo Alto: American West Publishing Company, 1975).

10. Issel and Cherny, *San Francisco*, 15, 24–25.

11. Elizabeth Bagwell, *Oakland: The Story of a City* (Novato: Presidio Press, 1982), 118–20. On the early years of Oakland's history see also Peter Conmy, *The Beginnings of Oakland, California, A. U. C.*, pamphlet (Oakland: Oakland Public Library, 1961).

12. Mellior Scott, *The San Francisco Bay Area: A Metropolis in Perspective* (Berkeley: University of California, 1959), 123.

13. Bagwell, *Oakland*, chs. 3 and 4; Mellior Scott, *San Francisco Bay Area*, ch. 8.

14. *Coast Review*, May 1902.

15. *California History*, 60 (Spring 1981), contains a series of articles devoted to the history of Los Angeles.

16. Robert Fogelson, *The Fragmented Metropolis: Los Angeles, 1850–1930* (Cambridge: Harvard University Press, 1967), chs. 3 and 4.

17. Fogelson, *Fragmented Metropolis*, ch. 4; the quotation is from p. 64. See also Billy M. Jones, *Health-Seekers in the Southwest* (Norman: University of Oklahoma Press, 1967).

18. William Friedricks, *Henry Huntington and the Creation of Southern California* (Columbus: Ohio State University Press, 1991).

19. Marc Weiss, *The Rise of the Community Builders: American Real Estate Developers, Urban Planners, and the Creation of Modern Residential Subdivisions* (New York: Columbia University Press, 1987), ch. 4.

20. Carl Abbott, *Portland: Planning, Politics and Growth in a Twentieth-Century City* (Lincoln: University of Nebraska Press, 1983), ch. 1; Percy Maddux, *City on the Willamette: The Story of Portland, Oregon* (Portland: Binfords and Mort, 1952); Paul Merriam, "Portland, Oregon, 1840–1890: A Social and Economic History" Ph.D. diss., University of Oregon, 1971, ch. 5; and Arthur Throckmorton, "The Role of the Merchant on the Oregon Frontier," *Journal of Economic History* 16 (December 1956): 539–50.

21. The articles in the *Oregon Historical Quarterly* 67 (June 1966) are devoted to the impact of the railroad on Portland.

22. Jones Jonasson, "Portland and the Alaska Trade," *Pacific Northwest Quarterly* 30 (April 1939): 131–44; and Alton Oviatt, "Pacific Coast Competition for the Gold Camp Trade of Montana," *Pacific Northwest Quarterly* 56 (October 1965): 168–74.

23. Abbott, *Portland*, 51; and E. Kimbark MacColl, *The Shaping of a*

City: Business and Politics in Portland, Oregon, 1885 to 1915 (Portland: The Georgian Press, 1976), chs. 10–14.

24. Neil Kimmons, "The Historical Development of Seattle as a Metropolitan Area," M.A. thesis, University of Washington, 1942; Janice Reiff, "Urbanization and the Social Structure: Seattle, Washington, 1852–1910," Ph.D. diss., University of Washington, 1981, chs. 1 and 2; and Roger Sale, *Seattle: Past to Present* (Seattle: University of Washington Press, 1976), chs. 1–3.

25. Robert Nesbit, *"He Built Seattle": A Biography of Judge Thomas Burke* (Seattle: University of Washington Press, 1961).

26. Jeannette Nichols, "Advertising and the Klondike," *Pacific Northwest Quarterly* 13 (January 1922): 20–26.

27. Alexander Norbert MacDonald, "Seattle's Economic Development, 1880–1910," Ph.D. diss., University of Washington, 1959, chs. 3 and 4; and MacDonald, *Distant Neighbors: A Comparative History of Seattle and Vancouver* (Lincoln: University of Nebraska Press, 1987), chs. 1–4.

28. MacDonald, "Seattle's Economic Development," ch. 9.

29. Diane Lindstrom, *Economic Development in the Philadelphia Region, 1810–1850* (New York: Columbia University Press, 1978), presents a valuable historical account of the interaction between one of America's developing cities and its hinterland.

30. On social mobility see Peter Decker, *Fortunes and Failures: White-Collar Mobility in Nineteenth-Century San Francisco* (Cambridge: Harvard University Press, 1978).

31. Issel and Cherny, *San Francisco*, 56. See also R. A. Burchell, *The San Francisco Irish, 1848–1880* (Berkeley: University of California Press, 1980), and Douglas Daniels, "Afro-San Franciscans: A Social History of Pioneer Urbanites, 1860–1930," Ph.D. diss., University of California, Berkeley, 1975.

32. Robert Knight, *Industrial Relations in the San Francisco Bay Area, 1900–1918* (Berkeley: University of California Press, 1960).

33. Issel and Cherny, *San Francisco*, 58–76.

34. Bagwell, *Oakland*, 87, 200–204; and Conmy, "Beginnings of Oakland," 45.

35. Fogelson, *Fragmented Metropolis*, 189.

36. *Ibid.*, ch. 7; the quotation is from p. 147.

37. Mansel G. Blackford, "The Lost Dream: Businessmen and City Planning in Portland, Oregon, 1903–1914," *Western Historical Quarterly* 15 (January 1984), 40.

38. *Ibid.*, 39–40.

39. Richard H. Engeman, " 'And So Made Town and Country One:' The Street Car and the Building of Portland, Oregon, 1872–1920," B.A. thesis, Reed College, 1969.

40. Reiff, "Urbanization and the Social Structure," ch. 3.

41. Blackford, "Civic Groups, Political Action, and City Planning in Seattle, 1892–1915," *Pacific Historical Review* 49 (November 1980), 557.

42. Reiff, "Urbanization and the Social Structure," chs. 4 and 5.

43. Allan Pred, *Urban Growth and City-Systems in the United States, 1840–1860* (Cambridge: Harvard University Press, 1980), 166–67. Eric Monkkonen, *America Becomes Urban: The Development of U.S. Cities & Towns, 1780–1980* (Berkeley: University of California Press, 1988), 79, also traces the development of a national urban network to the antebellum years.

44. Blake McKelvey, *The Urbanization of America, 1860–1915* (New Brunswick: Rutgers University Press, 1963), 34. See also Charles N. Glaab and A. Theodore Brown, *A History of Urban America* (London: Macmillan Company, 1967), which traces the "emergence of a national urban network" to the years 1860 through 1890 (p. 109).

45. San Francisco Real Estate Board, "Secretary's Report, December 31, 1911," unpaged, Carton 21, San Francisco Real Estate File, James D. Phelan Papers, the Bancroft Library, the University of California, Berkeley.

46. Robert G. Albion, *The Rise of New York Port, 1815–1870* (New York: Charles Scribner's Sons, 1939).

47. Wyatt Belcher, *The Economic Rivalry Between St. Louis and Chicago, 1850–1880* (New York: Columbia University Press, 1947).

48. For more detail on the economic changes occurring in California see Blackford, *The Politics of Business in California, 1890–1920* (Columbus: Ohio State University Press, 1977), ch. 1.

49. *Rambling Notes*, May 1893.

50. Rodman Paul, *Mining Frontiers of the Far West, 1848–1880* (New York: Holt, Rinehart, and Winston, 1963), 48–55.

51. *San Francisco Chamber of Commerce Journal*, September 1912.

52. San Francisco Chamber of Commerce, *Annual Report, 1909* (San Francisco 1909), 60; San Francisco *Examiner*, July 30, 1912.

53. *Oregon Journal*, May 2, 9, 1909. For later excursions see *Ibid.*, March 19, September 12, October 31, and November 8, 1911.

54. Blackford, *The Politics of Business in California* (Columbus: Ohio State University Press, 1977), 9–10.

55. San Francisco *Call*, September 9, 1911.

56. G. Allen Greb, "Opening a New Frontier: San Francisco, Los Angeles, and the Panama Canal, 1900–1914," *Pacific Historical Review* 47 (August 1978): 405–24.

57. *San Francisco Chamber of Commerce Journal*, June 1911.

58. *Oregon Journal*, February 13, 1911; *Oregon Daily Journal*, October 11, 27, November 20, 21, 1912.

59. Blackford, *Politics of Business*, 11.

CHAPTER 2

1. Mary Austin, "The Tremblor: A Personal Narration," *Out West*, 24 (June 1906), 500–501. For contemporary accounts of the earthquake and fire, see also San Francisco Board of Supervisors, *San Francisco Municipal Report for the Fiscal Year 1905-06* (San Francisco, 1908).
2. Judd Kahn, *Imperial San Francisco: Politics and Planning in an American City, 1897–1906* (Lincoln: University of Nebraska Press, 1979), ch. 6, offers an excellent analysis of the damage caused by the earthquake and fire. However, research by the city archivist of San Francisco suggests a death count as high as three thousand people. I am indebted to the anonymous reader for the press for the observation.
3. San Francisco Merchants' Association, *History of the Association, Programme for Progress, Constitution and By-Laws*, pamphlet, San Francisco, 1896, p. 3.
4. Roy Swanstrom, "Reform Administration of James D. Phelan, Mayor of San Francisco, 1897–1902," M.A. thesis, University of California, Berkeley, 1949, p. 64.
5. Frank Blackmar, "San Francisco's Struggle For Good Government," *Forum* 26 (January 1899), 570–72.
6. *Ibid.*, 577.
7. Kahn, *Imperial San Francisco*, ch. 3, and Swanstrom, "Reform Administration," 23–26, provide biographical sketches of Phelan. On his politics see William Issel, "Class and Ethnic Conflict in San Francisco Political History: The Reform Charter of 1898," *Labor History* 18 (Summer 1977): 341–59.
8. Kahn, *Imperial San Francisco*, 66.
9. Issel and Robert W. Cherny, *San Francisco, 1865–1932: Politics, Power, and Urban Development* (Berkeley: University of California Press, 1986), 152–53.
10. Stephen P. Erie, "How the Urban West Was Won: The Local State and Economic Growth in Los Angeles, 1880–1932," unpublished paper, p. 53.
11. Joan Elaine Draper, "The San Francisco Civic Center: Architecture, Planning, and Politics," Ph.D. diss., University of California, Berkeley, 1979, pp. 63–66.
12. San Francisco *Bulletin*, January 5, 1898.
13. San Francisco *Bulletin*, December 5, 1899, San Francisco *Chronicle*, November 21, 1899, and San Francisco *Examiner*, November 18,

26, and December 12, 1899, all in James Phelan Scrapbook 10, the James D. Phelan Papers, the Bancroft Library, the University of California, Berkeley.

14. San Francisco *Bulletin,* December 5, 1899, Phelan Scrapbook 10.
15. San Francisco *Examiner,* November 26, 1899, Phelan Scrapbook 10.
16. *Ibid.,* December 12, 1899.
17. *Ibid.,* December 3, 1899, Phelan Scrapbook 10.
18. San Francisco *Bulletin,* November 21, 1899, Phelan Scrapbook 10.
19. "The New San Francisco," broadside in Phelan Scrapbook 10.
20. San Francisco *Examiner,* December 3, 1899, Phelan Scrapbook 10.
21. The votes on the bonds were sewers: 21,250 yes, 820 no; hospital: 21,366 yes, 684 no; schools: 21,158 yes, 865 no—as reported in the San Francisco *Call,* December 30, 1899, Phelan Scrapbook 10.
22. San Francisco *Call,* December 30, 1899, Phelan Scrapbook 10.
23. San Francisco *Examiner,* Dcemeber 28, 1899, Phelan Scrapbook 10.
24. San Francisco *Post,* August 26, 1903, Phelan Scrapbook 17.
25. *Ibid.*
26. *Ibid.*
27. *Ibid.*
28. *Ibid.,* September 24, 1903, Phelan Scrapbook 17.
29. *Ibid.,* August 26, 1903, Phelan Scrapbook 17.
30. San Francisco *Chronicle,* September 30, 1903, and August 16, 1904, and the San Francisco *Evening Post,* August 26 and September 24, 1903, in Phelan Scrapbook 17.
31. Issel and Cherny, *San Francisco,* ch. 7.
32. Walton Bean, *California: An Interpretive History* (New York: McGraw-Hill, 1968), ch. 26, is a standard account of the origins of progressivism in San Francisco. For more detail see Bean, *Boss Ruef's San Francisco* (Berkeley: University of California Press, 1952); and Kahn, *Imperial San Francisco,* ch. 2.
33. The letter of invitation was reprinted in the San Francisco *Call,* January 13, 1904, Phelan Scrapbook 17.
34. San Francisco *Bulletin,* January 7, 1904, Phelan Scrapbook 17.
35. San Francisco *Call,* January 13, 1904, Phelan Scapbook 17, reprints the call to the meeting. The San Francisco *Bulletin,* January 16, 1904, Phelan Scrapbook 17, lists those at the founding meeting of the Association for the Improvement and Adornment of San Francisco (hereafter abbreviated as AIASF): the president of the Olympic Club, the vice-president of the H. S. Crocker Company, a major importer, the president of the Northern Commercial Company, the vice-president of the Crocker-Woolworth Bank, the manager of the St. Francis Hotel, the head of Louis & Taussig, a wholesale liquor dealer, the assistant to the president and the assistant traffic manager of the Santa Fe Railroad, the superintendent of the San Fran-

cisco Merchants' Exchange, the head of the Patek Company, wholesale butchers, John Partridge, an importer, the president of the Central Trust Company (who also was the president of the Merchants' Exchange), the manager of the Anglo-California Bank, a mining engineer and investor, the president of the Eastern Oregon Land Company, the dean of the Hastings College of Law, the president of the M. S. Keller Company, a clothing firm, the president of the Empire Mill and Mining Company (who also headed San Francisco Gas and Electric), several lawyers, and several men who listed their occupations in San Francisco's city directories as simply "capitalist."

36. San Francisco *Bulletin,* January 7 and 9, 1904, Phelan Scrapbook 17.

37. Board of Directors of the AIASF to the public, late April, 1904, in Phelan Scrapbook 17.

38. *Ibid.*

39. Thomas Hines, *Burnham of Chicago: Architect and Planner* (New York: Oxford University Press, 1974).

40. "First Annual Report of the President of the AIASF, July 1, 1905," Phelan Papers; "Second Annual Report of the President of the AIASF, March 15, 1906," Phelan Papers.

41. San Francisco *Bulletin,* May 5, 1904, Phelan Scrapbook 17.

42. Kahn, *Imperial San Francisco,* 85–86.

43. "Second Report . . . AIASF," 13.

44. "First Report . . . AIASF."

45. Daniel Hudson Burnham assisted by Edward H. Bennett, *Report on a Plan for San Francisco* (San Francisco: City of San Francisco, 1905), 35 (hereafter cited as the Burnham Plan).

46. Burnham Plan, 40.

47. Kahn, *Imperial San Francisco,* 90; Mellior Scott, *The San Francisco Bay Area: A Metropolis in Perspective* (Berkeley: University of California Press, 1959), 101–103.

48. *Burnham Plan,* 41.

49. Draper, "The San Francisco Civic Center," 89.

50. Burnham Plan, 41.

51. *Ibid.,* 112, 145.

52. For an overview of the diverse origins of city planning see William Wilson, *The City Beautiful Movement* (Baltimore: Johns Hopkins University Press, 1989), chs. 1–3. For additional detail see Harvey Kantnor, "The City Beautiful in New York," *New York Historical Quarterly* 57 (April 1973): 149–71; Michael McCarthy, "Chicago Businessmen and the Burnham Plan," *Journal of the Illinois State Historical Society* 62 (Autumn 1970): 228–56; Jon Peterson, "The City Beautiful Movement: Forgotten Origins and Lost Meanings,"

Journal of Urban History 2 (August 1976): 415–34; Mark Rose, "'There is Less Smoke in the District': J. C. Nichols, Urban Change, and Technological Systems," *Journal of the West* 25 (January–February 1986): 44–54; Stanley Schultz and Clay McShane, "To Engineer the Metropolis: Sewers, Sanitation, and City Planning in Late-Nineteenth-Century America," *Journal of American History* 65 (September 1978): 389–411; Wilson, "Harrisburg's Successful City Beautiful Movement, 1900–1915," *Pennsylvania History* 47 (July 1980): 213–33; Wilson, "J. Horace McFarland and the City Beautiful Movement," *Journal of Urban History* 7 (May 1981): 315–34; and Wilson, *The City Beautiful in Kansas City* (Columbia: University of Missouri Press, 1964).

53. Daniel Schaffer, ed., *Two Centuries of American Planning* (Baltimore: Johns Hopkins University Press, 1988), offers a solid introduction to the early history of American city planning.
54. Wilson, *City Beautiful*, 303.
55. *Ibid.*, 283.
56. "Second Annual Report of the . . . AIASF," 1–5; Scott, *San Francisco Bay Area*, 107.
57. Some even found time to laugh at their problems, as revealed in a piece of doggerel appearing in the San Francisco *Chronicle*, May 5, 1906:

> A wagon on a corner of the street;
> A swirl of dust, a whiff of frying meat;
> A stool that stands unsteady on its feet;
>
> A chophouse with its oft-repeated stew;
> And coffee—can we doubt its honest brew?—
> Are all that's left for hungry me and you.
>
> Ah, woe the day, when fire filled the air
> And burned the place of napery and chair—
> The joyous palace of printed bill of fare.
>
> Where you and I could take our time to dine
> And say the chef's creations were divine—
> And wash them down with beer—or even wine.
>
> But now, who in the bread line stands and begs,
> Or wanders till he's sore in heart and legs
> Knows when we'll see the end of ham and eggs?
> —"Lay of the Lost Restaurant"

58. A. D. Smith to Phelan, April 29, 1906, Carton 20, AIASF file, Phelan Papers.
59. Charles Lathrop to Phelan, April 30, 1906, Carton 20, AIASF File, Phelan Papers.
60. San Francisco *Chronicle*, May 4, 1906.
61. *The Merchants Association Review*, May, 1906.
62. San Francisco *Chronicle*, May 27, 1906.
63. Phelan to Thomas McCaleb, April 30, 1906, Phelan to S. W. Terry, May 4, 1906, Phelan to Mabelle Gilman, May 8, 1906, and Phelan to Andrew Crawford; all in Box 1 of the Phelan Papers.
64. Kahn, *Imperial San Francisco*, 132–35.
65. San Francisco *Chronicle*, May 5, 1906.
66. *Ibid.*, May 9, 1906.
67. *Ibid.*, May 22, 1906.
68. "Editorial," *Architectural Record*, 19 (June 1906), 436.
69. "Minutes of the Meeting of the Finance Subcommittee of the Committee on the Reconstruction of San Francisco, December 28, 1906," Phelan Papers.
70. San Francisco *Chronicle*, May 27 and 29, 1906.
71. AIASF to Board of Supervisors, May, 1906, Phelan Scrapbook 24.
72. San Francisco *Chronicle*, May 5, 1906.
73. Bean, *Boss Ruef's San Francisco*, ch. 8, examines the beginnings of the graft prosecutions.
74. *Merchants Association Review*, March, 1907.
75. *Ibid.*, May, 1907.
76. San Francisco *Chronicle*, May 22, 1906.
77. *Report of Marsden Manson to the Mayor and Committee on Reconstruction on the Improvements Now Necessary to Execute*, pamphlet, October 1906, pp. 4, 13.
78. *Merchants' Association Review*, June, 1909.
79. San Francisco *Chronicle*, April 6, 28, 30, 1908; and San Francisco *Examiner*, April 11, 19, May 1, June 5, 24, 1908.
80. San Francisco *Examiner*, April 24, 1908.
81. San Francisco *Chronicle*, April 23, 1908.
82. San Francisco *Chronicle*, April 15, 16, 23, 24, 29, May 11, 12, 1908; and San Francisco *Examiner*, April 12, 26, May 2, 10, 11, 1908.
83. Draper, "The San Francisco Civic Center," 99–103.
84. Resolutions in favor of the bonds by all of the organizations may be found in Carton 24, Civic Center File, Phelan Papers. See also San Francisco *Chronicle*, May 28, 1909.
85. "Civic Center Pamphlet Issued by the AIASF, June 22, 1909," unpaged, Phelan Scrapbook 24.
86. D. H. Burnham to Willis Polk, April 22, 1909, Phelan Scrapbook 24.
87. *Merchants' Association Review*, June, 1909.

88. San Francisco *Chronicle,* June 6, 1909.

89. *Ibid.,* May 31, 1909.

90. *Ibid.,* May 31, June 1, 5, 22, 1909.

91. *Ibid.,* June 23, 1909, reports the vote by district; the California Secretary of State, *Blue Book for 1909,* contains a map showing the political divisions of San Francisco.

92. *Merchants' Association Review,* October 1911. See also San Francisco *Call,* November 18, 1911, and San Francisco *Chronicle,* January 23, 1911.

93. Marc Weiss, *The Rise of the Community Builders: The American Real Estate Industry and Urban Land Planning* (New York: Columbia University Press, 1988).

94. San Francisco Chamber of Commerce, *Journal,* 1 (April 1911), 1.

95. San Francisco *Examiner,* July 30, 1912.

96. Chamber of Commerce, *Journal,* 1 (December 1911), 5.

97. William Sesnon, *Inaugural Address as President of the San Francisco Chamber of Commerce, January 21, 1913,* pamphlet (undated, no place of publication), p. 17.

98. *Merchants' Association Review,* April, 1910, and May, 1911. See also San Francisco *Call,* July 8, October 21, November 18, 1911, and March 23, 1912, and San Francisco *Examiner,* August 17, 1912.

99. San Francisco *Examiner,* August 17, 1912.

100. *Merchants' Association Review,* October 1909.

101. San Francisco Chamber of Commerce, *San Francisco, the Financial, Commercial, and Industrial Metropolis of the Pacific Coast,* pamphlet, San Francisco, 1915, p. 35.

102. *Merchants' Association Review,* January 1910.

103. San Francisco Real Estate Board, "Secretary's Report, December 31, 1911," unpaged, Carton 21, San Francisco Real Estate File, Phelan Papers.

104. San Francisco *Examiner,* April 15, 1912.

105. San Francisco *Call,* November 2, 1912.

106. San Francisco *Call,* August 5, 1911.

107. *San Francisco Chamber of Commerce Journal,* 1 (June, 1912), 14.

108. San Francisco *Examiner,* May 2, 1912.

109. San Francisco *Chronicle,* March 20, 1912.

110. San Francisco *Bulletin,* March 13, 1912.

111. San Francisco *Chronicle,* March 13, 1912.

112. San Francisco *Bulletin,* March 8, 1912; San Francisco *Call,* July 29, 1911; and San Francisco *Chronicle* March 8, 11, and 29, 1912.

113. Hamilton Wright, "Opening of the P-P E," *Overland Monthly* 65 (March 1915), 198.

114. *Improver,* July 1915, p. 17.

115. San Francisco *Bulletin,* August 1, 1914.

116. *Chamber of Commerce Activities*, March 25, 1915.
117. Edith Stellmann, "With the Crowd at the Panama–Pacific Exposition," *Overland Monthly*, 65 (June 1915), 514.
118. Alma Cook, "What Art Means to California," *California's Magazine* 1 (July 1916), 75.
119. *Chamber of Commerce Activities*, February 11, 1915.
120. Draper, "The San Francisco Civic Center," 231.
121. Bion Arnold, "Report on the Improvement and Development of the Transportation Facilities of San Francisco, March 31, 1913," San Francisco, 1913.
122. *Improver*, January 1915, p. 4.

CHAPTER 3

1. Elizabeth Bagwell, *Oakland: The Story of a City* (Novato: Presidio Press, 1982), 119.
2. *Ibid.*, 139.
3. Peter Commy, *The Beginnings of Oakland, California, A. U. C.*, pamphlet, Oakland, 1961, p. 44.
4. Mellior Scott, *The San Francisco Bay Area: A Metropolis in Perspective* (Berkeley: University of California Press, 1959), 80.
5. *Vote for Progress*, pamphlet, Oakland, 1892, unpaged.
6. *Ibid.*
7. *Ibid.*
8. *Does Oakland Need a Park?* pamphlet, Oakland, 1898, pp. 13–15.
9. "Broadside for Oakland Park Bonds, 1898," Bancroft Library, University of California.
10. Scott, *San Francisco Bay Area*, 86.
11. Oakland Board of Trade, *The Athens of the Pacific: Oakland, California*, pamphlet, Oakland, 1902, unpaged.
12. Mayor Frank Mott to the citizens of Oakland, undated, in Frank Mott Papers, Folder 2, Oakland Public Library.
13. Bagwell, *Oakland*, 178–89; Scott, *San Francisco Bay Area*, 123–25.
14. Bagwell, *Oakland*, 182.
15. *A Book of Combined Reports of the Various Departments of the City of Oakland, for the Fiscal Year 1905-06*, pamphlet, Oakland, 1906, pp. 72–73.
16. *A Review of the Municipal Activities in the City of Oakland, California, 1905–1915*, pamphlet, Oakland, 1915, p. 3.
17. Scott, *American City Planning Since 1890* (Berkeley: University of California Press, 1969), 65–69, presents a biographical sketch of Robinson; the quote is on p. 68.

18. William Wilson, *The City Beautiful* (Baltimore: Johns Hopkins University Press, 1989), 46.

19. Charles Mumford Robinson, *A Plan of Civic Improvement for the City of Oakland, California,* pamphlet, Oakland, 1906, p. 3 (hereafter cited as the Robinson Plan for Oakland).

20. *Ibid.,* 4–14.

21. *Ibid.,* 8, 9, 16.

22. *Ibid.,* 16–20.

23. Oakland *Tribune,* June 5, 1906.

24. Scott, *San Francisco Bay Area,* 129–30.

25. Oakland *Tribune,* January 8, 1907.

26. *Ibid.*

27. *Ibid.,* January 3 and 4, 1907. The newspapers list the businessmen supporting the park bonds.

28. *Ibid.,* January 14, 1907.

29. *Ibid.,* January 15, 1907.

30. Mayor Frank Mott, *Second Inaugural Address, April 1, 1907,* pamphlet, Oakland, 1907, pp. 1, 9.

31. Oakland Chamber of Commerce, *Oakland, California: The Coming Commercial City of the Pacific Coast,* pamphlet, Oakland, 1908, unpaged.

32. Oakland *Tribune,* January 10, 1907.

33. San Francisco *Examiner,* May 3 and 21, 1908.

34. Scott, *San Francisco Bay Area,* 132.

35. City of Oakland, "Report of the Playground Commission, July 30, 1910," 113–14.

36. City of Oakland, Department of Public Instruction, "School and Park Playgrounds of Oakland, August 1915," 1.

37. Mott, *Second Inaugural Address,* 14.

38. Oakland Chamber of Commerce, *Annual Reports, 1910–13,* pamphlet, Oakland, 1914.

39. Mott, *Second Inaugural Address,* 2.

40. Undated, unidentified newspaper clipping in the Oakland City Hall Clipping File, in the Oakland Public Library. See also San Francisco *Chronicle,* June 10, 1909.

41. National Register of Historic Places, "Nomination Form for the Oakland City Hall."

42. *Spectator,* May 13, 1911.

43. *Ibid.*

44. Oakland *Tribune,* November 10, 1913.

45. *Ibid.,* November 14, 1913; San Francisco *Examiner,* May 26, 1914.

46. San Francisco *Examiner,* May 26, 1914.

47. Oakland *Tribune,* March 5, 1914.

48. San Francisco *Chronicle,* June 13, 1914.

49. Werner Hegemann, *Report on a City Plan for the Municipalities of Oakland and Berkeley* (Oakland, 1915), unpaged preface (hereafter cited as the Hegemann Plan). On the Hegemann Plan see also Scott, *San Francisco Bay Area*, 160–64.
50. Hegemann Plan, 16.
51. *Ibid.*, 124.
52. Scott, *San Francisco Bay Area*, 164–67; Marc Weiss, *The Rise of the Community Builders: American Real Estate Developers, Urban Planners, and the Creation of Modern Residential Subdivisions* (New York: Columbia University Press, 1987).
53. Scott, *American City Planning*, 152.
54. *Ibid.*
55. *Ibid.*
56. Weiss, *Community Builders*, 86.
57. Los Angeles Chamber of Commerce, *Los Angeles, City and County*, pamphlet, 1915, p. 39.
58. For an extensive discussion of the Cox plan, see the supplement to the *California Outlook*, November 18, 1911. The quotation is from p. 6.
59. San Francisco *Examiner*, August 10, 1912.
60. Robert Fogelson, *The Fragmented Metropolis: Los Angeles, 1850–1930* (Cambridge: Harvard University Press, 1967), 260.
61. Robert Tracy, "John Parkinson and the Beaux-Arts City Beautiful Movement in Downtown Los Angeles, 1894–1935," Ph.D. diss., University of California, Los Angeles, 1982, pp. 194–98.
62. Weiss, *Community Builders*, 81.
63. Tracy, "John Parkinson," 286–87.
64. Fogelson, *Fragmented Metropolis*, 247.
65. *Ibid.*, chs. 10 and 11.
66. On Bartlett's background see Fogelson, *Fragmented Metropolis*, 191.
67. Dana Bartlett, *The Better City* (Los Angeles: Reuner Press, 1907), 27, 30–32.
68. Tracy, "John Parkinson," 199–204.
69. Charles Mumford Robinson, *The City Beautiful*, pamphlet, Los Angeles, 1909, p. 2 (hereafter cited as the Robinson Plan for Los Angeles).
70. *Ibid.*
71. *Ibid.*, 11–12.
72. *Ibid.*, 15.
73. *Ibid.*, 17.
74. *Ibid.*, 19.
75. *Ibid.*, 22.
76. *Ibid.*, 4–10.
77. *Ibid.*, 10.

78. *Ibid.*, 32.
79. *Ibid.*, 2.
80. *Ibid.*, 3.
81. Tracy, "John Parkinson," 207–208.
82. City of Los Angeles, Department of City Planning, *City Planning in Los Angeles: A History*, pamphlet, 1964, p. 4.
83. *California Outlook*, November 4, 1911, supplement, reprints the plan.
84. *Ibid.*, 20.
85. *City Planning in Los Angeles*, 6–8.
86. *California Outlook*, May 25, 1912.
87. Fogelson, *Fragmented Metropolis*, 265.
88. Steven P. Erie, "How the Urban West Was Won: The Local State and Economic Growth in Los Angeles, 1880–1932" unpublished paper, is the source of my information on Los Angeles's quest for water. The quotation is from p. 51.
89. *Ibid.*, 10.
90. *City Planning in Los Angeles*, 2–3.
91. Weiss, *Community Builders*, ch. 4.
92. *City Planning in Los Angeles*, 3.
93. Weiss, *Community Builders*, ch. 4.
94. *Ibid.*, 200; *City Planning in Los Angeles*, 8.
95. *City Planning in Los Angeles*, 9–11.
96. Weis, *Community Builders*, 95–96.
97. *Ibid.*, 98–101.
98. *City Planning in Los Angeles*, 10.
99. Fogelson, *Fragmented Metropolis*, 249.
100. Scott L. Bottles, *Los Angeles and the Automobile: The Making of the Modern City* (Berkeley: University of California Press, 1987); and Mark Foster, "The Model-T, the Hard Sell, and Los Angeles's Urban Growth: The Decentralization of Los Angeles during the 1920s," *Pacific Historical Review*, 44 (November 1975): 459–84.
101. Scott, *Metropolitan Los Angeles: One Community* (Los Angeles: Haynes Foundation, 1949), 165.
102. Richard Barsness, "Railroads and Los Angeles: Quest for a Deep Water Port," *Southern California Quarterly*, 47 (December 1965): 379–94; Robert Weinstein, "The Million-Dollar Mud Flat," *American West*, 6 (January 1969): 33–44.
103. San Francisco *Call*, September 9, 1911.
104. Scott, *San Francisco Bay Area*, 139–40.
105. San Francisco *Call*, November 25, 1911.
106. San Francisco *Chronicle*, February 4, 1911.
107. Mansel G. Blackford, *Politics of Business in California, 1890–1920* (Columbus: Ohio State University Press, 1977), 10.

108. *Ibid.,* 11.
109. Erie, "How the Urban West Was Won," 38.
110. *Ibid.,* 41.

CHAPTER 4

1. On the history of city planning in Seattle, see Padraic Burke, "The City Beautiful Movement in Seattle," M.A. thesis, University of Washington, 1973; J. M. Neil, "Paris or New York: The Shaping of . Downtown Seattle, 1903–14," *Pacific Northwest Quarterly* 75 (January 1984): 22–33; William Wilson, *The City Beautiful Movement* (Baltimore: Johns Hopkins University Press, 1989), chs. 7 and 10; and Wilson, "How Seattle Lost the Bogue Plan: Politics versus Design," *Pacific Northwest Quarterly* 75 (October 1984): 171–80.
2. See Wilson, "The Seattle Park System and the Ideal of the City Beautiful," in Daniel Schaffer, ed., *Two Centuries of American Planning* (Baltimore: Johns Hopkins University Press, 1988).
3. Donald Roberts, "A Study of the Growth and Expansion of the Seattle Municipal Government," M.A. thesis, University of Washington, 1943, p. 161.
4. Superintendent of Parks, "Advisory Letter," in Seattle Board of Public Works, Department of Parks, *Annual Report, 1894,* (Seattle 1895), 5–6.
5. Seattle Park Commission, "Report for 1893," 1–2.
6. *Ibid.;* and Seattle Board of Park Commissioners, *Annual Report, 1892* (Seattle, 1893), 4–8.
7. *Ibid.*
8. "Advisory Letter . . . 1894," 3.
9. Seattle Board of Park Commissioners, *Parks, Playgrounds and Boulevards of Seattle, Washington* (Seattle, 1909), reprints Olmsted's report.
10. Burke, "City Beautiful," ch. 2; and Roberts, "Seattle Municipal Government," ch. 8.
11. Seattle *Municipal News,* January 9, 1915; and Seattle *Post-Intelligencer,* March 3, 1912.
12. Seattle *Municipal News,* October 5, 1912. On political reform in Seattle in the Progressive Era, see Mansel G. Blackford, "Reform Politics in Seattle in the Progressive Era, 1902–1916," *Pacific Northwest Quarterly* 59 (October 1968): 177–85; and Lee Pendergrass, "The Formation of a Municipal Reform Movement: The Municipal League of Seattle," *Pacific Northwest Quarterly* 66 (January 1975): 13–25.
13. Seattle Playground Association, *The Playground Movement of Seattle,* pamphlet, Seattle, 1909, p. 8.

14. A ward-by-ward and precinct-by-precinct tabulation of votes for issues and candidates in Seattle's elections is available in the *Journal of the Proceedings of the City Council of the City of Seattle* located in the Seattle City Clerk's office. See the *Proceedings* for March 6, 1906, March 3, 1908, March 8, 1910, and March 5, 1912 for park bond votes.

15. J. C. Olmsted, "Diary Notes, May 21, 1903," File 5, Box 1, Olmsted Brothers Papers, Manuscript Division, University of Washington Library, Seattle.

16. Olmsted to A. J. Blethen (president, Board of Regents, University of Washington), June 4, 1903, File 1, Box 1, Olmsted Papers.

17. On the history of the exposition, see George Frykman, "The Alaska-Yukon-Pacific Exposition, 1909," *Pacific Northwest Quarterly* 53 (July 1962): 89–99. On the exposition's relationship to Seattle's economic interests, see Barry McMahon, "Seattle's Commercial Aspirations as Expressed in the Alaska-Yukon-Pacific Exposition," M.A. thesis, University of Washington, 1960.

18. Frykland, "The Alaska-Yukon-Pacific Exposition," 92–93.

19. *Pacific Northwest Commerce,* September, November, and December, 1909.

20. "Minutes of the Meetings of the Washington State Chapter of the American Institute of Architects (hereafter cited as WSCAIA), March 3, 1900, March 27, 1902, May 4, July 6, and December 12, 1904, and February 7, 1906," in WSCAIA Papers, Manuscript Division, University of Washington Library.

21. *Ibid.,* April 3, 1907.

22. *Ibid.,* February 6, April 3, December 12, 28, 30, 1907; January 16, March 5, 1908.

23. *Proceedings of City Council,* March 6, 1908; Seattle *Post-Intelligencer,* March 2, 1908.

24. "Minutes . . . WSCAIA, January 28, 1909," WSCAIA Papers.

25. Municipal Plans League, "Constitution and By-Laws," WSCAIA Papers.

26. "Minutes . . . WSCAIA, November 26, 1909," WSCAIA Papers.

27. Seattle *Post-Intelligencer,* February 22, 1910.

28. "Minutes . . . WSCAIA, December 1, 1909," WSCAIA Papers.

29. Seattle *Daily Times,* February 25, 1910.

30. Seattle *Post-Intelligencer,* February 6, 1910.

31. *Ibid.,* March 6, 1910.

32. *Ibid.,* February 27, 1910.

33. *Ibid.,* March 6, 1910.

34. Seattle *Daily Times,* March 2, 1910; and Seattle *Union Record,* February 19 and 26, 1910.

35. R. H. Thomson to Virgil Bogue, July 6, 1910, File 3, Box 1, R. H.

Thomson Papers, Manuscript Division, University of Washington Library.

36. *Proceedings of City Council,* March 8, 1910.
37. See Blackford, "Reform Politics in Seattle During the Progressive Era."
38. *Ibid.,* 182.
39. *Pacific Northwest Commerce,* 2 (April 1910), 21.
40. The Municipal League, which would soon emerge as the strongest champion of the Bogue Plan, was composed of middle-class professionals and businessmen. While well-educated and financially secure, they were not part of Seattle's upper-class business elite. See Pendergrass, "The Formation of a Municipal Reform Movement," and Norbert MacDonald, "The Business Leaders of Seattle, 1880–1910," *Pacific Northwest Quarterly* 50 (January 1959): 1–13.
41. See *Plan of Seattle: Report of the Municipal Plans Commission, Submitting Report of Virgil G. Bogue Engineer* (Seattle, 1911), p. 10 (cited hereafter as the Bogue Plan).
42. Bogue to Thomson, September 2, 1910, and Thomson to Bogue, June 25, July 30, and September 1, 1910, all in File 3, Box 1, Thomson Papers.
43. On Bogue's career see Burke, "City Beautiful," 77–79, and Robert Nesbit, *"He Built Seattle": A Biography of Judge Thomas Burke* (Seattle: University of Washington Press, 1961), 236–37.
44. Wilson, "How Seattle Lost the Bogue Plan," 173. On Thomson's career see Grant Redford, ed., *That Man Thomson* (Seattle: University of Washington Press, 1950).
45. "Minutes . . . WSCAIA, July 22, 1910 [?]," WSCAIA Papers.
46. Thomson to Olmsted, June 25, 1910, and Thomson to H. B. Swope, January 9, 1911, both in File 3, Box 1, Thomson Papers.
47. Seattle *Post-Intelligencer,* September 29, 1910.
48. "Minutes . . . WSCAIA, October 5, 1910, and September 26, 1911," WSCAIA Papers; *Pacific Northwest Commerce,* September, 1910, May and July, 1911; Seattle *Post-Intelligencer,* June 17, 1910, and July 14, 1911; Thomson to Norwood Brocket (the secretary of the Municipal Plans Commission), September 3, 10, and 23, 1910, File 3, Box 1, Thomson Papers; and Thomson to Bogue, April 5, 1911, File 4, Box 1, Thomson Papers.
49. Bogue Plan, 21–33, 112–37.
50. *Ibid.,* 54–111. See also Padraic Burke, "Struggle for Public Ownership: The Early History of the Port of Seattle," *Pacific Northwest Quarterly,* 68 (April 1977): 60–71.
51. Bogue Plan, 34–40. On the location of the civic center, see also Neil, "Paris or New York," 25; and Wilson, "How Seattle Lost the Bogue Plan," 174.

52. Bogue Plan, 41–53.
53. *Ibid.*, 21–33, 57–60, 112–37.
54. *Ibid.*, 34.
55. *Ibid.*, 44–45.
56. *Proceedings of City Council,* January 9, October 9 and 30, 1911.
57. *Pacific Northwest Commerce* 4 (May 1911), 1 and 17.
58. "Minutes . . . WSCAIA," April 5, 1911.
59. Thomson to C. J. Smith, September 25, 1911, File 4, Box 1, Thomson Papers.
60. Seattle *Union Record,* March 19, 1910.
61. *Pacific Northwest Commerce,* November and December 1909, various issues; Seattle *Daily Times,* February 25, and March 5, 1910; and Seattle *Post-Intelligencer,* February 26, 1910.
62. Neil, "Paris or New York."
63. *Proceedings of the City Council,* March 8, 1910.
64. *Ibid.*, May 23, September 6, 12, November 8, 1910; "Minutes . . . WSCAIA, June 13, October 5, 1910," WSCAIA Papers; *Municipal League News,* July 1, 15, 1911 (hereafter cited as *MLN*); and *Town Crier,* December 15, 1910.
65. *MLN,* August 19 and 26, 1911.
66. *Proceedings of the City Council,* November 8, 1910 and September 8, 1911.
67. *MLN,* August 19, 1911, January 6, 20, February 10, 1912; Pacific Northwest Society of Civil Engineers, "Proceedings," July 1911 and January 1912; Seattle *Daily Times,* February 28, 1912; and Seattle *Post-Intelligencer,* March 5, 1912.
68. *MLN,* October 21, 1911, January 20, February 10, 1912; Seattle *Post-Intelligencer,* February 20, 25, 26, March 4, 1912; Seattle *Daily Times,* March 5, 1912; and *Town Crier,* May 20, 1911.
69. *MLN,* July 1, 1911; and Seattle *Post-Intelligencer,* March 5, 1912.
70. Reprinted in *MLN,* February 10, 1912.
71. *MLN,* January 20, 1912.
72. *Ibid.*, July 1, 1911.
73. Seattle *Post-Intelligencer,* March 5, 1912.
74. *MLN,* February 10, 1912.
75. *Town Crier,* May 20, 1911.
76. *MLN,* September 2, 1911.
77. *The Bogue Plan Question,* pamphlet, Seattle, 1912, available at the main Seattle public library.
78. *MLN,* November 25, and December 16, 1911.
79. Seattle *Union Record,* February 24 and March 2, 1911.
80. Burke, "Struggle for Public Ownership," and H. M. Chittenden, "The Harbor Island Episode: A History," 1915 typewritten manuscript, the Northwest Collection, the University of Washington.

81. *Oregon Journal,* October 28, 1909.
82. Seattle *Post-Intelligencer,* February 24, 1912.
83. *Town Crier,* October 15, 29, November 12, 1910.
84. *Proceedings of City Council,* March 5, 1912.
85. *MLN,* January 20, 1912.
86. Seattle *Post-Intelligencer,* March 4, 1912.
87. Minnie Frazier to Joe Smith, January 12, 1912, File 12, Box 8, Joe Smith Papers, Manuscript Division, University of Washington.
88. Stephen Erie, "How the Urban West Was Won: The Local State and Economic Growth in Los Angeles, 1880–1932," unpublished paper.
89. Blackford, "Reform Politics in Seattle," 184–85.
90. Seattle *Post-Intelligencer,* October 20, 1912.
91. Seattle *Daily Times,* October 7, 1912.
92. *Seattle Municipal News,* September 7, 1912.
93. Neil, "Paris or New York," 29–32.
94. Seattle *Municipal News,* July 11, August 1, 15, 22, December 5, 1914.
95. "Minutes . . . WSCAIA, February 7, March 6, 1912, January 8, 1913," WSCAIA Papers; *MLN,* March 16, May 11, 1912; Seattle *Municipal News,* April, 1915; and *Town Crier,* February 10, March 30, 1912.
96. "Minutes . . . WSCAIA, March 5, 1913," WSCAIA Papers; and Seattle *Municipal News,* June 28, 1912.
97. Hines, *Denny's Knoll,* chs. 3–6.
98. On the impact of the automobile on city planning nationally, see Mark Foster, *From Streetcar to Superhighway: American City Planners and Urban Transportation, 1900–1940* (Philadelphia: Temple University Press, 1981).
99. Seattle *Times,* February 25, 1945.
100. *Ibid.,* September 17, 1972.

CHAPTER 5

1. George Muleside to the mayor of Portland, 1912, File 117–7, Portland City Council Documents, Portland City Archives, Portland Oregon.
2. *Portland Chamber of Commerce Bulletin,* June, 1912.
3. On the history of city planning in Portland, see Carl Abbott, "Greater Portland: Experiments with Professional Planning, 1905–1925," *Pacific Northwest Quarterly* 76 (January 1985): 12–21; Abbott, *Portland: Planning, Politics, and Growth in a Twentieth-Century City* (Lincoln: University of Nebraska Press, 1983); Ellis Lawrence, "The City Planning Movement in Portland," *The Architect and Engineer* 56 (March 1919): 77–80; Arthur McVoy, "A History of City Planning in Portland, Oregon," *Oregon Historical Quarterly* 46 (March 1945):

3-21; and Alice Miles, "City Planning in Portland," B.A. thesis, Reed College, 1940.

4. *Oregon Journal*, November 8, 1909.

5. Portland Park Commission, *Annual Report, 1901* (Portland, 1902), 11.

6. E. Kimbark MacColl, *The Shaping of a City: Business and Politics in Portland, Oregon 1885-1915* (Portland: Georgian Press, 1976), 268.

7. Portland Park Board, *Annual Report, 1903* (Portland, 1904), 15; this report reprints Olmsted's report. See also Abbott, *Portland*, 59-60.

8. Park Board, *Report, 1903*, 13, 20, 25, 31.

9. *Oregon Journal*, March 21, 1906.

10. *Ibid.*, March 3, 1906.

11. *Ibid.*, November 12, 1909.

12. People's Institute Club to Portland Park Board, January 16, 1908, reprinted in Portland Park Board, *Annual Report, 1909* (Portland, 1910), 8-9.

13. *Oregon Journal*, March 14, 1911.

14. Portland Superintendent of Parks to the Mayor of Portland, September 30, 1912, Portland City Documents, Portland City Archives.

15. *Oregon Journal*, May 1, 1907.

16. MacColl, *The Growth of a City*, 273.

17. *Ibid.*, May 13, 18, 28, June 4, 1907. No voting records broken down by area of the city have survived to the present day.

18. Thomas Strong to the editor of the *Oregonian*, January 26, 1907, File 4, Thomas Strong Papers, Oregon Historical Society, Portland.

19. Portland *Labor Press*, April 22, 1909.

20. Portland Park Board, *Annual Report, 1913* (Portland, 1914), 12-13. See also Abbott, *Portland*, 60-61.

21. Abbott, *Portland*, 35-44.

22. F. G. Young, "Suggestions for a Congress of Industry and Commerce, As a Means to Realize the Central Idea of the Lewis and Clark Centennial," *Quarterly of the Oregon Historical Society* 2 (June 1901), 206.

23. Lawrence Pratt, *I Remember Portland, 1899-1915* (Portland: no publisher listed, 1965), 63.

24. Abbott, *Portland*, 42.

25. Park Board, *Report, 1903*, 7.

26. MacColl, *Shaping of a City*, 270.

27. *Oregon Journal*, March 5, 1906, prints the membership list.

28. *Ibid.*, March 13, 1906.

29. *Ibid.*, May 30, 1909.

30. *Ibid.*, May 9, 1907.

31. *Ibid.*, March 6, 8, 1906, May 14, 1907, October 27, 1909; Portland *Labor Press*, April 13, 1911.

32. *Oregon Journal,* May 30, 31, June 5, 8, 9, 1909; Portland *Labor Press,* May 27, 1909.
33. *Oregon Journal,* December 8, 1909.
34. *Ibid.,* May 6, 1907.
35. *Ibid.,* May 5, 1909.
36. *Ibid.,* December 18, 1909.
37. Portland Art Association and Portland Architectural Club, *Year Book: Second Annual Exhibition* (Portland, 1909), unpaged.
38. Portland *Labor Press,* June 23, 1908.
39. Lawrence, "City Planning," 77; Miles, "City Planning," 10, 19.
40. *Oregon Journal,* October 28, 29, November 7, 13, December 1, 1909.
41. *Ibid.,* December 8, 1909, February 12, 1911.
42. *Ibid.*
43. *Oregon Journal,* December 1, 1909, prints a list of subscribers to the planning fund. See also Bourne's incoming and outgoing correspondence for November 1909 in the Jonathan Bourne Papers, Special Collections, University of Oregon Library.
44. *Oregon Journal,* December 14, 1909. See also Abbott, "Greater Portland," 15; and Miles, "City Planning," 12.
45. MacColl, *Shaping of a City,* chs. 12–14.
46. *Oregon Journal,* November 14, 1911.
47. *Ibid.,* September 11, 1911.
48. Marshall Dana, *The Greater Portland Plan of Edward H. Bennett* (Portland, 1912), 5 (hereafter cited as Bennett Plan).
49. Bennett Plan, 18, 30; Abbott, "Greater Portland," 16.
50. Bennett Plan, 9–12.
51. *Ibid.,* 27.
52. *Ibid.,* 25–26.
53. *Ibid.,* 20–21, 33, 38–39.
54. *Ibid.,* 5, 34.
55. *Ibid.,* 6.
56. *Ibid.,* 5.
57. *Oregon Journal,* March 26, 1911.
58. *Ibid.,* February 28, March 20, 21, 23, 26, October 30, 31, 1911; and Portland *Labor Press,* March 30, 1911.
59. "Election Returns for June 5, 1911," Portland Sample Ballots Scrapbook, Portland City Auditor's Office.
60. *Oregon Journal,* September 15, 1911. Among those at the meeting were representatives of the Portland Press Club, the Progressive Business Men's Club, the Rotary Club, the East Side Businessmen's Club, the North Albina Improvement Association, the Irvington Club, the Art Association, the Mount Tabor Improvement Association, the Portland Realty Board, the South Portland Boosters, the Steel Bridge Push Club, the Cedar Hill Club, the East Harrison

Street Improvement Club, the Myrtle Street Club, and the Wood-lawn Improvement Club.

61. *Oregon Journal,* November 14, 1911.
62. *Ibid.*
63. *Ibid.,* November 15, 22, December 2, 15, 17, 1911; *Oregon Daily Journal,* August 21, 30, September 25, October 6, 11, 26, 1912; and Abbott, "Greater Portland," 16.
64. *Ibid.,* October 11, 1912.
65. GPPA, untitled leaflet, fall 1912.
66. *Oregon Journal,* October 31, 1912; Portland *Labor Press,* February 1, March 28, April 18, May 23, September 5, October 17, 24, 1912.
67. "Election Returns for November 2, 1912," Portland Sample Ballots Scrapbooks.
68. *Oregon Daily Journal,* September 12, 20, 23, October 1, November 4, 1912.
69. Portland *Labor Press,* October 17, 1912.
70. "Election Returns for November 2, 1912," Portland Sample Ballots Scrapbook.
71. *Greater Portland,* February, 1913.
72. *Ibid.*
73. *Ibid.*
74. *Ibid.;* East Side Business Men's Club to the Mayor of Portland, November 1, 1911, City Council Documents; and *Oregon Daily Journal,* November 21 and 26, 1912.
75. *Greater Portland,* February and March, 1913.
76. *Portland Chamber of Commerce Bulletin,* December, 1912.
77. A copy of the letter to ministers may be found in the "Minutes of the Park Board Meeting, May 29, 1913," Portland City Auditor's Office.
78. "Election Returns for June 2, 1913," Portland Sample Ballots Scrapbook.
79. *Greater Portland,* March, 1913.
80. *Oregon Daily Journal,* October 14, 1912.
81. Richard Engeman, "'. . . And So Made Town and Country One': The Streetcar and the Building of Portland, Oregon, 1872–1920," B.A. thesis, Reed College, 1969.
82. Abbott, "Greater Portland," 16.
83. McVoy, "History of City Planning," 4.

CHAPTER 6

1. For a survey of the roles businessmen played in America's progressive movement see Mansel Blackford and K. Austin Kerr, *Busi-*

ness Enterprise in American History (Boston: Houghton Mifflin, second edition, 1990), ch. 7. For a more detailed account see Robert Wiebe, *Businessmen and Reform: A Study of the Progressive Movement* (Cambridge: Harvard University Press, 1962).

2. William Wilson, *The City Beautiful Movement* (Baltimore: Johns Hopkins University Press, 1989), 302.

3. Wilson, *City Beautiful*, especially ch. 13.

4. See M. Christine Boyer, *Dreaming the Rational City: The Myth of American City Planning* (Cambridge, Mass.: MIT Press, 1983).

5. Wilson alludes to the importance of intercity rivalry, without developing its importance, at several points. See his *City Beautiful*, 29. Stanley K. Schultz, *Constructing Urban Culture: American Cities and City Planning, 1800–1920* (Philadelphia, 1989), 187–88, also notes that "Nineteenth-century city leaders generally viewed their communities as competing with others for urban growth and new population. A reputation for excellence in public works and healthfulness served local boosters well in the wars of urban imperialism."

6. For overviews see Thomas McCraw, *Prophets of Regulation* (Cambridge: Harvard University Press, 1984); and James Q. Wilson, ed., *The Politics of Regulation* (New York: Basic Books, 1980).

7. See Guy Alchon, *The Invisible Hand of Planning: Capitalism, Social Science, and the State in the 1920s* (Princeton: Princeton University Press, 1985); Robert M. Collins, *The Business Response to Keynes, 1929–1964* (New York: Columbia University Press, 1981); and Ellis W. Hawley, *The New Deal and the Problem of Monopoly* (Princeton: Princeton University Press, 1966).

8. Wilson, *City Beautiful*, 302–3.

9. *Ibid.*, 292.

INDEX

Abrahamson, Hugo, 66
Ainsworth, John C., 131–32, 135, 137–38, 144, 152
Alaska-Yukon-Pacific Exposition, 103–4, 108, 121, 155
Allen, Charles, 118
American Civic Association, 48
Arnold, Bion, 62, 90
Association for the Improvement and Adornment of San Francisco, 38–41, 46, 49–50, 54, 110, 137, 152
Austin, Mary, 31

Backus, Frank, 80
Bank of California, 15, 60
Barth, Gunther, 9
Bartlett, Dana, 85
Bebb, Charles, 105
Bennett, Edward, 40–43, 54; prepares a city plan for Portland, 138–50

Bennett Plan for Portland, 128–29, 139–50
Blethen, Joseph, 112
Bogue, Virgil, 98, 110–16
Bogue Plan for Seattle, 98, 111–27, 146
Bourne, Jonathan, 136, 138
Boyer, Christine, 7
Burnham, Daniel, 40–47, 51–52, 54, 60, 106, 136
Burnham Plan for San Francisco, 41–52, 54, 56–59, 73, 80, 88, 98, 112
Businessmen: and planning in America, 3; support city planning, 1–2, 152–54, 158–59. *See also* individual cities
Byrne, J. W., 39

Cahill, B. J. S., 35, 42–43
Chandler, Alfred D., Jr., 10

187